THE
FILM
MARKETING
HANDBOOK

THE FILM MARKETING HANDBOOK

A PRACTICAL GUIDE TO MARKETING STRATEGIES FOR INDEPENDENT FILMS

EDITED BY JOHN DURIE
WRITTEN BY ANNIKA PHAM NEIL WATSON

 MEDIA BUSINESS SCHOOL

ISBN: 84-88773-00-5

Printed in Great Britain by:
BAS Printers Limited, Over Wallop, Hampshire

Design by Carroll and Brown Limited, London NW6 6RA
Cinema Photographs courtesy of Artificial Eye, London

CONTENTS

SECTION 4 MARKETS AND FESTIVALS 53–78

SECTION 5 FILM DISTRIBUTION IN EUROPE 79–158

LIST OF CHARTS

ECU rate and other currency conversions dated 18 August 1993

ACKNOWLEDGEMENTS

The authors would like to thank the following film industry professionals who set aside time from often hectic schedules for interviews which provided invaluable source material for this book.

Thierry Abel

Daniel Battsek

Karl Baumgarten

Simona Benzakein

Albert Bert & Sons

Patrizia Biancamano

Monique Bondil

Stephen Burdge

Martin Butterworth

Norma Cairns

Hélène Cardis

Isabel Carrasco

Maurizio della Casa

Philippe de Chaisemartin

Denis Chateau

Adriana Chiesa

Bo Christensen

Roberto Cimpanelli

Duncan Clark

Dennis Davidson

John Dick

Erwin Dietrich

Eliane Dubois

Lena Enquist

Andi Engel

Stan Fishman

Peter Fornstam

Tullio Galleno

Dany Geys

Andrés Vicente Gómez

Bruno Gosse

Thomas Halbere

Joseph Helfgot

Alexandre Heylen

Paco Hoyos

Bernadette Icovic

Gilles Jacob

Ralph Kamp

Chris Koppelmeier

Jean Labadie

Pierre Ange LePogam

Elena Lloyd

Michel Luel

San Fu Maltha

Enrique Gonzalez Macho

Jean-René Marchand

Pandelis Mitropoulos

Wendy Palmer

Valerio de Paolis

Alberto Pasquale

Tracy Payne

Gerhard Pedersen

Pedro Perez

Peter Philipsen

Sandro Pierotti

Claude-Eric Poiroux

Peter Refn

Renate Rose

Arnaud Rouvilloix

Mike Ryan

Bertil Sandgren

Rosemary de Siati

Bill Stephens

Ute Schneider

Hy Smith

Per Tengblad

Simon Ubsdell

Tharci Vanhuysse

Jan Verheyen

José Vicuña

Herman Weigel

Wim van Wouw

Anke Zindler

The authors would also like to acknowledge the generous assistance, encouragement and support by a number of other people throughout the gestation of this book. At the Media Business School, the former general manager Gudie Lawaetz and in particular Antonio Saura for their enthusiastic backing and nurturing of the project. Also Fernando Labrada, the new general manager of the MBS, as well as Nadine Luque, Isabel de las Casas and all the other members of the staff who provided unstinting support and helpful suggestions throughout. Without their backing, this project could not have reached fruition.

John Chittock and the editorial team at Screen Digest kindly allowed us to reproduce statistical data from their publication.

Denise Brown and the staff at Carroll & Brown in London provided sterling support and worked beyond the call of duty to ensure that the production of this book met printing deadlines. As well as Denise, we would like to extend special thanks to Alan Watt, Jules Selmes, Rowena Feeny, Wendy Rogers, indexer Susanne Atkin. Julian Newby and Luci Collings who provided particularly efficient copyediting and proofing services and Lorraine Baird, production consultant.

Finally, we would like to thank Holde Lhoest, head of the MEDIA Programme, who was responsible for creating the initiative which made this project possible in the first place.

FOREWORD

Getting a film onto a cinema screen is a process comprised of many distinct but inter-linked stages, including financing, production and distribution, each of which requires its own specialised talent and expertise.

However, there is one common link which unites all the different stages of the life of a film, and that is marketing. The target audience may change at each stage – when a film is being sold to the industry, the marketing is aimed at international distributors, whereas when a film is finally distributed, the goal is to reach the cinema going public. But whether the task is the preparation of a synopsis designed to raise the interest of potential financiers, the arranging of a screening to industry and press at the Cannes Film Festival or making a trailer for the general public, marketing is involved at each step.

Thus for every type of film, ranging from large mainstream releases to specialised arthouse pictures, a marketing strategy must be created and executed, using a set of established tools. The film business is dependent on persuading distributors to pay out money to acquire rights to pictures and enticing the public to buy cinema tickets. The marketing strategy for a film plays a crucial role in determining the success of this process.

In The Film Marketing Handbook, we start from the basic concepts of feature film marketing, and attempt to show how to create marketing strategies which will use these tools in the most effective way at each stage of a film's life.

It is often assumed that the success of film marketing is dependent on the strength of a single creative idea. While not disputing the importance of such ideas, this book tries to demonstrate how they will only be effective if they are incorporated into a focused but flexible marketing plan, based on a realistic budget. Film marketing is not an exact science, but proper planning which allows sufficient time for the preparation of the necessary materials will greatly increase the chances of attaining the desired goal and help minimise the risk of costly mistakes.

This book has evolved from the work of the Media Business School (MBS), an initiative of the Media 95 Programme created by the European Community to assist the development of the European audiovisual industry. One of the primary objectives of the MBS is to create a forum in which European film makers can benefit from training, whatever stage of their career they have reached. This book forms part of that effort.

The Film Marketing Handbook focuses primarily on the marketing and distribution of independent films in Europe, although the sections on international sales, markets and festivals will be applicable to any independent film, regardless of country of origin, size or budget. The text is based on interviews with over 80 senior figures involved in all aspects of film marketing in 14 different European countries. We have tried to distil a wide range of approaches into a coherent shape, while maintaining a flavour of the different perspectives that we encountered during our research across the different territories.

The effective marketing of European films is crucial given that US films dominate the marketplace in most European countries. If European films are to survive, and perhaps win back some of the share lost to the Americans, then their makers must develop marketing strategies which will enable their films to be sold more effectively both to distributors and to the general public.

The Film Marketing Handbook is designed to allow readers to dip in and out of its various sections, each of which addresses marketing at a different stage of a film's life. In effect, it is rather like a cookbook with you, the reader, as the chef, selecting the particular ingredients that you believe will work most successfully for your film. Since every film is composed of a different set of elements, the overall effect is like trying a new recipe each time, and it will be impossible to predict the results until the film reaches its final customer – the paying public. I wish you good cooking.

John Durie

FILM MARKETING: WHAT IS IT AND WHY IS IT NECESSARY ?

❝ The goal of film marketing is to maximise the audience for a film and, by extension, its earning potential. ❞

While it is important to be aware of the tools of film marketing, such knowledge is of limited use unless accompanied by a detailed understanding of how to use these tools in an effective way, as part of a coherent, cost-effective strategy.

In the international film industry, awareness and knowledge of the importance of film marketing has increased considerably in the last few years. This is partly because of the escalating costs of releasing films, which has meant that companies are eager to ensure that money is being spent in the most cost-effective way. The increasing sophistication of many marketing campaigns means that unless a given film avails itself of an effective marketing strategy its chances of earning its money back in a crowded marketplace are considerably diminished.

WHAT IS THE TARGET AUDIENCE?

This book is concerned with the marketing and distribution of independent films as opposed to those handled by the **Hollywood majors**. For independent pictures, there are, in effect, two target audiences for the marketing process, each of which relates to a different stage of the film.

The first target audience is the **international distributor**, also known as the buyer, since without a distributor the picture will not be released. Once the film has been sold to the distributor, the target audience becomes the cinema goer, who must be persuaded to see the film.

WHY DOES A FILM NEED TO BE MARKETED?

There is a section of the film industry which argues that a film does not need to be marketed, since it is art, the intrinsic value of which will be instinctively recognised by its audience. A film, it is argued, is not a product like soap powder which needs to be actively marketed in order to persuade the public to buy it. The very word "product" is felt to demean the artistic status of a film. While such an argument is often a manifestation of the passion which people inside the industry feel for films, it runs the risk of ignoring certain key aspects of the way in which films are put together and of ignoring the workings of the marketplace.

Most films are only produced after a lengthy period of gestation, during which considerable energy is expended in seeking to ensure that they will be attractive to a target audience, however that audience is defined. In such terms, a film does have the status of a product, since like many other products it passes through a phase of research and development, during which the aim is to orientate it towards a particular market.

Selling to international buyers or to the public is ultimately dependent on creating something which people are prepared to risk money to distribute, or which people are prepared to pay to see at the cinema. Indeed, even the most esoteric film is made for a paying audience, be it at a cinema, or through renting or buying a video or on broadcast television. As such, a film is a leisure activity which uses people's disposable income. Marketing a film to the public involves competing not only with other films, but with other types of leisure activity vying for disposable income.

The premise that forms the backbone of this book is that the goal of marketing is to maximise the audience for a film and, by extension, its earning potential. There is no intention to prescribe the kinds of films which could or should be made, rather, the intention is simply to underline throughout that a film is a business, in which companies are driven by the need to make a profit. Marketing is an essential part of this process.

WHAT IS FILM MARKETING?

As is stressed throughout this book, film marketing is any element that assists a film in reaching its target audience at any time throughout its life. In order to achieve this, a marketing strategy must be constructed, a strategy which creates marketing tools and uses them in the most effective manner possible.

As such, the marketing strategy will incorporate elements as diverse as print designs (e.g. posters), *trailers* and *showreels*, publicity, advertising, promotion and merchandising.

A FILM AS A PROTOTYPE

In the film industry what is often being sold is an idea, a concept which the buyer wants to believe is going to be exciting, enjoyable – desirable by an audience, big or small. Every film, whatever its inherent merit, is a unique creation, since it will contain a mix of different elements which have never before been put together in that way, and which will never be repeated in quite that way again. Thus, each film may be defined as a prototype. When people buy a product which is new to them, they may first engage in the process of sample testing (for example, trying on several pairs of jeans before purchasing). In the case of toothpaste or soft drinks, the consumer may buy several different brands before settling on a favourite. By contrast, an audience cannot closely compare a new film with another existing product and will not be able to sample it fully, except by paying to see it. Therefore a film can be defined as a one-off purchase, not a repeat purchase like many other products.

> **"A film can be defined as a one-off purchase. "**

The audience searches for perceived hallmarks of quality and may, of course, decide to see a certain film based on the name of the director, the star or the genre of the film. However, because a film is dependent on the combination of a large number of variables, such a decision does not guarantee consumer satisfaction. To minimise the chances of wasting time and money on a bad film, the audience may also seek information prior to purchase through word of mouth, reviews and advertising.

Before being sold to the general public, however, the film has to be sold to the international distributor, and here, time is critical.

THE SHELF LIFE OF A FILM

A company selling films to international distributors has only a limited amount of time in which to convince them to buy. This period – the film's *shelf life* – will climax with the screening of the finished film. Few films increase their value once they have been screened. The goal of the company representing the film is to sell a project at the time when its value is at its maximum. This may be prior to the completion of the film, or it may be once the film is finished.

When a film is released to the general public it also has a limited shelf life. It is rare that a film increases its box-office value once it has been released. The focus of the marketing strategy will be the release date of the film, with the aim of maintaining interest for as long as possible following its debut in the marketplace.

In order to plan an effective marketing strategy it is crucial to have an understanding of the overall environment in which the campaign will be executed. The following section examines the changing nature of the European marketplace and why these changes have made marketing so crucially important.

THE CHANGING PATTERN OF CINEMA GOING IN EUROPE

❝ The European film industry has been forced to acknowledge that it must work harder to attract people into the cinema. ❞

During the last 30 years, the nature of cinema going in Europe has undergone dramatic changes. Whereas a visit to the cinema was once regarded as a mass activity which the public would undertake with relatively little persuasion, an explosion in the variety of other available leisure pursuits means that getting people to pay to see films requires much greater effort. The rapid growth of new television channels and an increase in available airtime has also meant that consumers now have access to a cheap and convenient alternative source of audiovisual entertainment.

Faced with these challenges, the European film industry has been forced to acknowledge that it must work harder to attract people into the cinema. As such, the marketing of films has assumed a much greater importance, accompanied by a marked increase in sophistication.

Five key changes in patterns of cinema going have had a direct impact on the nature and scope of film marketing:

- *Decline in cinema admissions*

- *Decline in the number of screens*

- *The rise of ancillary media*

- *Changing leisure patterns*

- *The decline in the share of European films*

DECLINE IN CINEMA ADMISSIONS

According to figures from the UK-based monthly trade publication Screen Digest, in 1960, 2.9 billion cinema tickets were sold in the countries which now comprise the European Community. By 1990, the number of tickets sold in those same countries had fallen to just 564 million (see chart p.19).

The same source reports that in 1990 each European visited the cinema on average 1.7 times – just one-sixth of the figure for 1960 – and spent an average of $9 (ECU8). By contrast, in the US, the habit of cinema going has remained relatively strong with 4.2 visits per year per capita, with an average spend per visitor of $21 (ECU18.8) (see chart p.20).

Cinema admissions in the EC and North America (1950-1992)
(figures in millions)

	1950	1960	1970	1980	1982	1985	1988	1990	1991	1992	% change 82-92	91-92
Belgium	116.36	79.56	30.39	20.65	20.53	17.87	15.22	17.10	16.90	16.55	−19.4	−2.1
Denmark	52.16	43.92	23.86	15.90	14.30	11.30	9.96	9.62	9.22	8.65	−39.5	−6.2
France	370.73	354.67	184.40	174.80	201.90	175.00	124.70	121.90	117.50	115.90	−42.6	−1.4
Germany	487.40	604.80	167.40	143.80	124.50	104.20	108.90	102.50	119.90	105.92	−14.9	−11.7
Greece	....	61.20	128.60	42.99	35.30	23.00	17.00	13.00	10.00	6.50	−81.6	−35.0
Ireland	46.00	41.00	20.00	9.50	7.00	4.50	6.00	7.40	8.08	8.20	+17.1	+1.5
Italy	661.55	744.80	525.00	241.90	195.36	123.10	93.13	90.70	88.60	83.60	−57.2	−5.6
Lux	....	4.50	1.30	0.80	0.80	0.70	0.50	0.54	0.61	0.60	−24.8	−1.3
Neth'nds	63.93	55.44	24.14	25.58	20.49	15.30	14.80	14.60	14.90	13.70	−33.1	−8.1
Portugal	20.60	26.59	28.00	30.80	27.31	19.00	13.70	11.00	11.80	12.00	−56.1	+1.7
Spain	....	370.00	330.86	176.00	155.90	101.10	69.60	78.50	79.10	83.30	−46.6	+5.3
UK	1,395.80	500.80	193.00	101.00	64.00	72.00	84.00	97.92	101.27	103.65	+61.9	+2.4
Total EC	3,214.53	2,887.28	1,656.95	983.72	867.39	667.07	557.51	564.78	577.88	558.57	−35.6	−3.3
Canada	....	107.70	80.80	89.00	97.30	80.60	75.70	81.00	71.60	82.20	−15.5	+14.8
US	3,017.50	1,304.50	920.60	1,021.50	1,175.40	1,056.10	1,084.80	1,056.60	968.30	964.20	−18.0	−0.4

source : Screen Digest

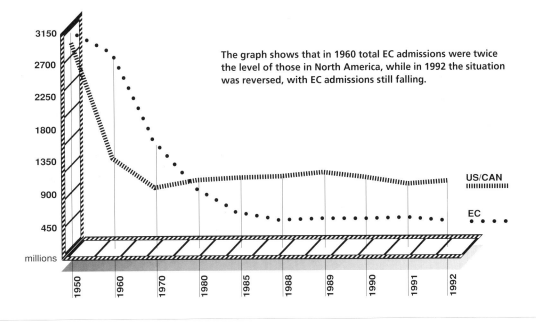

The graph shows that in 1960 total EC admissions were twice the level of those in North America, while in 1992 the situation was reversed, with EC admissions still falling.

Average box office spend per capita in EC countries and North America
(figures in US dollars)

	1980	1981	1985	1986	1987	1988	1989	1990	1991	1992
Belgium	6.64	5.48	4.75	6.07	6.95	6.34	6.73	8.42	8.10	8.26
Denmark	8.40	7.51	5.51	7.43	9.36	7.68	8.52	8.99	8.15	8.74
France	11.53	11.15	10.47	12.40	12.75	10.73	11.33	13.24	12.56	13.94
Germany	7.51	6.77	5.15	6.62	8.43	7.54	7.64	9.08	9.61	9.98
Greece	4.79	....	3.13	....	3.62	4.33	4.85	5.19	6.36	3.50
Ireland	12.34	....	4.91	....	5.48	6.47	6.99	8.93	9.69	10.16
Italy	7.65	6.62	5.22	7.52	8.15	6.88	7.82	9.31	9.07	10.29
Luxembourg	4.17	....	6.25	....	6.11	5.84	5.30	7.95	8.29	....
Netherlands	7.08	6.05	3.86	4.86	6.36	5.62	6.30	6.67	6.43	6.64
Portugal	2.83	3.03	1.91	2.57	2.69	2.55	2.08	2.73	2.94	3.70
Spain	7.58	7.10	4.26	4.76	6.03	5.22	6.49	7.40	7.43	9.74
UK	6.06	4.60	3.13	3.69	5.54	6.13	6.38	8.18	8.32	10.84
Average EC	7.76	6.68	5.38	6.54	7.84	7.05	7.60	9.02	8.91	10.21
Canada	9.71	....	8.67	....	10.34	11.64	13.72	13.79	12.60	13.78
US	12.07	12.89	15.67	15.79	17.77	18.63	21.04	20.99	18.97	19.06

source : Screen Digest

THE NUMBER OF SCREENS

This decline in admissions also led to the closure of many cinema screens throughout Europe. Between 1960 and 1990, a 60% decrease in screen capacity was registered across Europe, according to Screen Digest (see chart p.21). In many cases it became harder for people to find a cinema in their own neighbourhood, which served as a further disincentive for going to see films. However, the building of *multiplexes* in Europe, which began during the mid-1980s, together with the introduction of more flexible ticket pricing, has gone some way to providing new cinema capacity in certain countries such as Germany and the UK. In the UK this has been accompanied by a substantial rise in cinema admissions.

THE RISE OF ANCILLARY MEDIA

The growth of the video market and the deregulation of television have also had a major impact on patterns of film consumption in Europe. This has resulted in an overall expansion in the demand for filmed entertainment.

Number of cinema screens in EC countries and North America

	1950	1960	1970	1980	1991	1992
Belgium	1,415	1,506	714	508	431	411
Denmark	447	462	374	475	322	317
France	5,213	5,821	4,381	4,540	4,441	4,402
Germany	3,962	6,950	3,673	3,422	3,686	3,630
Greece	170	560	1,034	1,103	350	300
Ireland	290	220	237	163	173	164
Italy	7,946	10,393	11,560	8,453	3,100	3,000
Luxembourg	39	52	31	20	18	17
Netherlands	488	559	435	523	418	416
Portugal	448	437	485	423	200	207
Spain	3,950	6,922	6,911	4,096	1,806	1,807
UK	4,583	3,034	1,529	1,576	1,789	1,845
Total EC	28,951	36,916	31,364	25,302	16,734	16,516
US	19,016	16,999	13,750	17,590	24,570	25,105

source : Screen Digest

The chart indicates that since 1960, the number of cinema screens in EC countries has fallen by more than half, with the sharpest fall registered in Italy. Since the introduction of multiplexes in Europe during the mid-1980s, some countries, notably the UK, have recorded a rise in the overall number of cinema screens.

VIDEO

Video first emerged as an important medium for viewing feature films during the early 1980s. Initially, it was the rental of videos which was the principal source of revenue from the sector. By 1992, video accounted for around 41.1% of the total expenditure on films by the public in Europe, while receipts from theatrical box office accounted for about 34.7% of revenue, with *pay-TV* – which involves consumers paying a monthly subscription to receive a particular television channel – accounting for the remainder (see chart p.22).

Share of expenditure on filmed entertainment by media, in different countries (figures in %)

PAY-TV

	1988	1989	1990	1991	1992
Benelux	13.14	14.52	16.07	17.23	22.37
France	43.92	45.20	43.53	44.78	48.22
Austria	0.81	1.13	2.71	2.85	7.99
Greece	....	....	0.66	1.18	1.50
Italy	....	....	....	1.00	5.44
Portugal	....	....	....	....	....
Scandinavia	1.99	3.45	8.88	16.07	20.35
Spain	....	....	1.27	10.89	13.33
Switzerland	11.32	10.62	9.91	11.90	11.95
UK/Ireland	4.00	3.88	14.82	22.76	25.15
Europe	12.33	13.43	16.95	20.83	24.14
Japan	....	....	0.08	1.17	4.10
US	25.34	24.79	24.61	24.98	24.84

VIDEO

	1988	1989	1990	1991	1992
Benelux	41.64	41.89	41.54	40.00	39.61
France	16.07	18.86	24.28	25.64	23.06
Austria	57.46	55.38	55.26	54.51	54.29
Greece	66.37	60.31	40.60	32.92	24.93
Italy	27.43	29.61	34.45	36.30	37.87
Portugal	61.84	70.23	70.96	64.73	66.07
Scandinavia	58.81	56.37	55.21	48.75	45.67
Spain	60.37	60.97	55.72	45.22	46.12
Switzerland	34.49	40.36	39.12	35.86	37.15
UK/Ireland	68.69	70.08	61.08	53.77	49.68
Europe	46.88	46.93	45.74	42.79	41.10
Japan	68.54	70.49	70.15	71.25	69.34
US	43.93	44.40	46.30	47.49	48.26

CINEMA

	1988	1989	1990	1991	1992
Benelux	45.22	43.60	42.39	42.78	38.02
France	40.00	35.94	32.19	29.58	28.72
Austria	41.73	43.49	42.03	42.65	37.73
Greece	33.63	39.69	58.74	65.90	73.57
Italy	72.57	70.39	65.55	62.70	56.68
Portugal	38.16	29.77	29.04	35.27	33.93
Scandinavia	39.20	40.17	35.91	35.18	33.98
Spain	39.63	39.03	43.01	43.89	40.55
Switzerland	54.19	49.02	50.98	52.23	50.90
UK/Ireland	27.31	26.03	24.10	23.47	25.17
Europe	40.78	39.64	37.30	36.39	34.77
Japan	31.46	29.51	29.77	27.59	26.56
US	30.73	30.81	29.10	27.54	26.90

source : Screen Digest

The charts left show that the share of consumer expenditure on film accounted for by pay-TV in Europe doubled between 1988 and 1992. The proportion of expenditure claimed by video has been falling since 1989, partly as a result of the impact of pay-TV.

Rental is still the primary source of revenue from video in many European countries, but the purchase of tapes by the consumer, known as video **sell-through**, has become increasingly prevalent, although special-interest tapes, rather than feature films, have become the driving force of this sector.[1] The sell-through sector is particularly strong in France and Italy.

As in the rest of the world, most EC countries have adopted a 6-12 month **window** between theatrical and video release dates in order to ensure that theatrical revenues do not suffer as a result of the growth of video. However, even with such a window in operation, consumers know that if they wait a few months after the theatrical release they can view a film on video for much less than the cost of a cinema ticket – cost being widely cited by the public as a deterrent against visiting the cinema.

TV AND PAY–TV

Alongside video, the deregulation of television, brought about as European governments allowed private operators to challenge state monopolies, also created an additional medium for the viewing of feature films. Between 1988 and 1992, the number of European pay-TV subscribers increased from 2.9 million to 8.2 million. In particular, the French pay-TV service Canal +, which also has stakes in pay services in Belgium, Germany and Spain, has been a driving force in the growth of such channels. BSkyB in the UK and Telepiu in Italy also operate pay-film channels, which have contributed to the overall increase in spending on filmed entertainment in Europe (see chart p.25).

The types of film which succeed in these ancillary markets are invariably the same as those that work in the cinema – the so-called A titles, whose principal ingredients are recognised stars and quality production values. Since the marketing campaign for the cinema release of a film has a relatively high profile, it will also act as an essential tool in creating consumer interest in the film not just for the cinema, but also in these ancillary markets.

1 In 1992, among the new titles for release on sell-through, feature films accounted for 32.9% of the market in the UK, 40.9% in Germany. In France they took 60.5% of the market in the first quarter of 1993. (Source: Mediabase, Brussels.)

Even with the anticipated development of new technologies – such as **video-on-demand**, which will enable films to be delivered via the telephone to the home – theatrical marketing will probably remain the key to other markets because of its high profile.

However, despite the strength of the ancillary markets, a visit to the cinema is likely to retain its appeal for many people because the experience of going to see a film on the big screen is an event that cannot be replicated by viewing a film on the small screen.

CHANGING LEISURE PATTERNS

As well as competing with a variety of different media, cinema going also faces challenges from a growing number of other leisure pursuits which are competing for the time and money of the public. Although working hours have decreased in Europe over the last few years, a new leisure economy has emerged in which activities such as eating out, sports and going to nightclubs have become increasingly important (see chart below).[2]

Average weekly household expenditure on leisure items in the UK (1991)

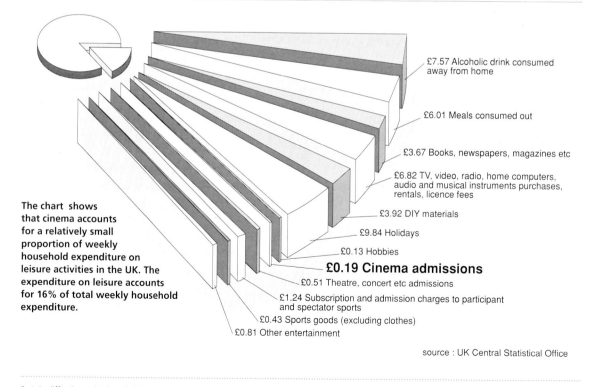

£7.57 Alcoholic drink consumed away from home

£6.01 Meals consumed out

£3.67 Books, newspapers, magazines etc

£6.82 TV, video, radio, home computers, audio and musical instruments purchases, rentals, licence fees

£3.92 DIY materials

£9.84 Holidays

£0.13 Hobbies

£0.19 Cinema admissions

£0.51 Theatre, concert etc admissions

£1.24 Subscription and admission charges to participant and spectator sports

£0.43 Sports goods (excluding clothes)

£0.81 Other entertainment

The chart shows that cinema accounts for a relatively small proportion of weekly household expenditure on leisure activities in the UK. The expenditure on leisure accounts for 16% of total weekly household expenditure.

source : UK Central Statistical Office

2 It is difficult to obtain reliable information on the share of total leisure time claimed by cinema across Europe. However, the graph above provides information on the share of leisure time held by cinema going in the UK.

Average spend per capita on filmed entertainment in Europe, Japan and the US (figures in US dollars)

	1988	1989	1990	1991	1992
Benelux	13.06	14.81	17.40	16.64	18.64
France	26.82	31.51	41.12	42.46	43.80
Gfr/Aus	19.44	19.04	23.14	23.80	25.37
Greece	12.86	12.22	8.83	9.66	8.01
Italy	9.49	11.11	14.20	14.46	15.98
Portugal	6.68	6.98	9.39	8.79	8.25
Scandinavia	26.98	30.28	34.84	34.51	35.94
Spain	13.16	16.63	17.20	16.93	18.28
Switzerland	26.05	29.84	33.73	32.70	34.23
UK/Ireland	22.51	24.63	34.13	35.78	37.41
Europe	18.06	20.13	25.06	25.61	26.99
Japan	32.75	34.31	32.15	35.56	36.01
US	58.90	65.71	68.77	68.87	71.83

source : Screen Digest

The chart shows that spend per capita on filmed entertainment in the US consistently outstrips that in Europe. The Japanese also spend more per capita than the Europeans.

THE DECLINE IN THE SHARE OF EUROPEAN FILMS

Between 1981 and 1991, the decline in cinema attendances was mirrored by a sharp decline in the popularity of European films. Meanwhile, films originating in the US have maintained their level of popularity, so that the net effect has been to increase their percentage share of the box office at the expense of European films. By 1991, films of US origin had increased their share of the national box office to as much as 80% in many countries, while in the UK the figure had reached 93% (see chart p.26). Even in France, where a system of state support and tax incentives for the film industry has helped to sustain a strong domestic industry, US films accounted for 58.7% of the total box office in 1991.

A wide variety of reasons have been offered for the diminishing popularity of local films in the various territories. Some observers point to a decline in productions rooted in a specific culture while others argue that European production has failed to adapt to changing audience tastes. It is not the purpose of this book to adjudicate between the various arguments. But it is clear that if European films are to have any chance of succeeding in an extremely competitive market, then expertise in film marketing is of vital importance.

Share of EC markets held by films according to their country of origin (1991)

Country	% Share held by US films	% Share held by indigenous films	% Share held by other films
Belgium	82	3.0	15.0
Denmark	70	16.0	14.0
France	58.7	30.1	11.2
Germany	77	11.0	12.0
Greece	88	7.0	5.0
Ireland	91.5	2.0	6.5
Italy	68	24.0	8.0
Luxembourg	67	3.0	30.0
Netherlands	83	4.0	13.0
Portugal	85	1.0	14.0
Spain	75	10.0	15.0
UK	93	5.5	1.5

% Share held by US films

source : Screen Digest

The chart above shows that US films command a substantial share of national markets throughout the EC, notably in the UK. In France, the strength of the indigenous industry means that US films hold a rather lower share of the domestic market.

INTERNATIONAL SALES

" The selling of pictures is a specialised business, and one that requires a comprehensive knowledge of distributors and market trends around the world. "

The task of marketing often begins with the conception of the film when the producer first has to sell the idea to potential financiers who will put up the money to fund the project.

In Europe, a few projects will be entirely financed by commercial investors putting up money in return for a share of the profits, together with funds from one of the many subsidy systems that are available to the European producer.[1] But in most cases, because such funds alone will not be sufficient to cover the entire costs of the picture, the producer will need to engage the services of a sales company or **international sales agent**. Such a company will either employ a process known as **pre-sales**, by which funds are raised for the film before it is completed, or help sell it once it has been finished and screened, a process known simply as **sales**.

Like all aspects of film marketing and distribution, the ultimate goal of international sales is the maximisation of profit, and to achieve that end sales companies use well-established, sometimes complex, financing mechanisms. As such, it is essential that if producers choose to finance or part-finance a picture through the sales route, they should use an established sales agent rather than attempt the task themselves or simply hand the job to enthusiastic friends in the industry.

Selling pictures is a specialised business and requires a comprehensive knowledge of distributors and market trends. Novice producers who ignore established procedures and conduct their own international sales could fast find themselves both out of their depth and out of pocket.

This chapter will outline the most effective procedures for attracting the interest of a sales agent, before explaining how the latter subsequently markets the film in such a way as to maximise the interest of international distributors, also known as buyers.

But before doing so, it is necessary to explain the environment in which the international sales agent operates. We will start by outlining the way in which the financing of many pictures in Europe differs from the methods often used in the US.

FINANCING AND DISTRIBUTING FILMS: AN OVERVIEW

US FILMS

From a business perspective, the key difference between most European and US films is the manner in which they are financed. In the US, the majority of *mainstream* films released in the cinema are developed, financed and distributed by one of the major Hollywood studios.[2] In some cases, the film will also be shown in a cinema chain in which the respective Hollywood major has an interest.[3] The majors, which are all owned by large conglomerates, have sufficient capital resources to handle all stages of the film making process under one roof.

This ability to handle the entire process of film making, from the development of the original idea through to the distribution of the finished picture, gives the studios enormous marketing advantages. From the earliest possible moment, and certainly by the time an initial version of the script is ready, the marketing and distribution arms of the studio will be involved in putting together ideas for the film's marketing campaign.

In some instances, the overseas distribution arms of these film companies may be asked to contribute ideas on casting and even to comment on the script to ensure that its idiosyncrasies will be acceptable to foreign audiences. The studio will also attempt to calculate the potential box office of the film based on the previous track record of its stars, director and genre in certain territories.

INDEPENDENTS

There are few, if any, companies anywhere in the world that have the financial resources to compete with the Hollywood majors and which are able to develop an initial idea, finance the subse-

1 The key funds would include the European Script Fund, which provides conditionally refundable loans to aid development, and Eurimages, which assists co-productions. Tax-driven schemes such as the French system of creating Sociétés pour le Financement de l'Industrie Cinématographie et Audiovisuelle (SOFICAs) are also an important source of funding in some countries. Such systems usually enable those putting money in pictures originating in that particular country to write off part of their investment against tax.

2 The term Hollywood majors usually refers to the following companies: Columbia Pictures, Walt Disney, MGM, Paramount, 20th Century Fox, Universal, Warner Brothers.

3 However, unlike distribution, where the film is handled exclusively by one major, when it comes to screening the film in the cinema, the production company will wish to have the picture shown on as many screens as possible, not just in the cinema chain in which it has an interest.

quent production and handle the worldwide distribution of the resulting film under one roof. The majors have long-established operations which have ready access to talent, and the costs of entry for a company which sought to create an operation to rival the majors would be astronomical.

A number of major *independent* companies, such as Carolco and Morgan Creek, are involved, like the majors, in developing pictures. However, these films will usually be distributed in a different way. In many instances, a studio will acquire *theatrical rights* for the US, giving it the right to distribute the film to cinemas in that territory. Other rights may also be included in the deal.

In return for these rights, some of the costs of development may be borne by the Hollywood majors. To raise the remaining production money, such companies will usually seek to sell the films to foreign distributors around the world, either through their own sales arm or using a company that specialises in the international sales of feature films.

EUROPEAN FILMS

A handful of European producers and/or directors are able to finance their pictures with the help of the studio system. The British producer David Puttnam has a *first look* arrangement with Warner Brothers, in which the US studio provides development money to Puttnam's company Enigma Productions, and in return has first refusal to invest in any project that comes to fruition, along with specified distribution rights. Jean-Jacques Annaud has a similar type of deal under which Sony finances his pictures.

Most films originating in Europe are produced without the help of the Hollywood studio system, although the US majors do sometimes finance European pictures. The finance for their development and production is assembled from a variety of sources by independent producers. In many cases, the financing package involves a complex mix of public subsidies, funds invested for tax reasons, and investment from private companies. Distribution rights are sold separately, although the money raised from this sale may be used to help finance the production of the film.

As a result, in Europe the company that develops a film will rarely be the same one that distributes it, and the investors in a film may be independent of either entity.

The kind of long-term strategic planning undertaken by the US majors, in which the marketing department will be consulted virtually from the inception of a project, is rare elsewhere, because a distributor may not be in place at such an early stage. But in Europe, even though distributors may acquire rights to a picture well before it starts shooting, the process of creating a marketing and distribution campaign is often left until the production is underway or, more likely, until the film is completed. As a result, there is often simply too little time to create an effective marketing campaign which will be attractive to distributors.

Starting on the planning for the marketing campaign of a film as early as possible, even though the film may not have even started shooting, is vital. In practice it is a point routinely ignored by many European producers. Allocating sufficient time to plan and implement the campaign can often mean the difference between success and failure.

Such neglect seriously undermines the ability of European films to compete with their US counterparts at the box office and may have been a contributory factor in the increasing grip exerted by US films in terms of market share at the European box office.[4]

WHAT IS A SALES AGENT?

Since there are few opportunities for independent films to be financed and distributed by a single entity, a number of mechanisms have been developed which are designed to expedite the process of raising funds for production. As most European films are produced independently, they will tend to rely on one of these mechanisms as a means to raise funding.[5] The most common such mechanism involves using an international sales company, or sales agent, which sells or *licences* the films to distributors in each international territory.[6]

There are two different types of sale: that which is made before the film is completed and screened, known as a pre-sale, and that which is made once the film is completed and has been shown – a straight sale. As a rule, it is easier to pre-sell English-language films because distributors view these films as entailing less risk, whereas they see non-English-language films as pictures which

---

4 See Section Two: The Changing Pattern of Cinema Going in Europe.

5 Independently produced films in territories around the world, including the US, will also tend to use similar mechanisms, particularly that of pre-sales.

6 International sales agents are also sometimes referred to as international distributors. However, in strict terms, an international distribution company is a group engaged in the distribution of films to cinema chains in several different countries (see Section Five: Film Distribution in Europe).

require careful handling in order to reach the kind of specialised audiences who will be attracted to such material.

Non-English-language films can usually be pre-sold in their home territory. But generally they can only be pre-sold abroad if they feature an internationally known star such as Gérard Depardieu, or a top European director such as Bernardo Bertolucci. In continental Europe there is an acute shortage of stars who can cross borders and no more than a handful of directors whose names are sufficient to pre-sell a picture. If the film does not have one of these ingredients it is often necessary to wait until it is completed before attempting to sell the film to most territories around the world.

Pictures at the lowest end of the budget scale (whether English-language or non-English-language) will be expected to recoup their costs primarily from their home territory. In such instances, foreign sales will simply be an additional revenue stream rather than a determining factor in whether the film gets made at all.

> **It is vital for a producer to try to ensure that a sales agent is willing to take on some of the risk involved in trying to finance a picture.**

It is vital for a producer to try to ensure that a sales agent is willing to take on some of the risk involved in trying to finance a picture. The sales agent should be prepared to bear some of the costs of marketing the film to international distributors, rather than the burden of this falling entirely on the producer. In this way, the sales agent will have some financial risk in the film and therefore an extra incentive to sell it on.

Many of the leading international sales companies are based in London, which is a primary source for the financing of English-language pictures. They include companies such as J&M Entertainment, Majestic Films and Television International, and CiBy 2000. These companies tend to deal with English-language pictures, although most of them have handled prestige films made in other languages. But other European sales companies, such as French cinema giant Gaumont, Germany's Futura/Filmverlag der Autoren and Spain's Iberoamericana, also pre-sell pictures to the international market, often on the basis of the director's name and the story content.

After the film is released, the sales agent will also collect monies from distributors, on behalf of the producer, and will act as the producer's "caretaker" for the duration of the licensing period – usually 15 years. Sales agents have considerably more negotiating power than producers, because they are often able to tell the distributor that they will hold back delivery of any future pictures until they are paid all outstanding money. By contrast, producers

> **" Sales agents have considerably more negotiating power than producers, because they are often able to tell the distributor that they will hold back delivery of any future pictures until they are paid all outstanding money. "**

will not usually have completed pictures which they can use as bargaining chips in this way.

Securing a sales agent – particularly a good one – is one of the primary roles of the producer. As the international sales community is relatively small according to Mike Ryan, co-chairman of J&M Entertainment, there are about 20 international sales agents worldwide who can substantially enhance the power of a project – competition for their services is therefore fierce. Approaching them professionally will be discussed in the next section.

HOW PRE-SALES WORK

The key elements in the system of pre-sales are the sales agent, a bank and the distributors in the key territories throughout the world. For the majority of films these key territories may be defined as the US, Canada, Australia, France, Germany, Italy, Japan, Korea, Scandinavia, Spain and the UK.

It is not the purpose of this book to explain all the possible scenarios which can occur when a film is pre-sold. The financing of films, particularly independent pictures, can be extremely complex, especially since there is no such thing as standard product in the film industry and so every picture tends to be financed in a different way.

In the simplest pre-sales scenario a sales agent acting on behalf of the producer undertakes to sell a film to as many distributors worldwide as possible, prior to the film commencing *principal photography*. Each distributor undertakes to advance a specified sum of money to the sales agent, once they take delivery of the completed film together

> **" The financing of films, particularly independent pictures, can be extremely complex. "**

with certain materials such as *poster-ready artwork* and a trailer. The funds that the distributor commits to advance on delivery are known as the *minimum guarantee*.

Once the film is released in a particular territory the returns to the distributor from the film may exceed the original minimum guarantee paid. In this instance, the distributor will start paying additional revenues known as *overages* to the sales agent at an agreed rate. This will be divided between the sales agent and the producer, according to a specified formula in each case.

CROSS-COLLATERALIS-ATION

The redistribution of earnings from theatrical distribution by the respective distributor in each territory can be made more complex by a common practice known as *cross-collateralisation*. The cross-collateralisation of rights means that the distributor offsets any losses incurred from theatrical distribution of the film against profits from sales in other media such as video or television, before distributing to the sales agent, and then the producer, their share of the profits.

Cross-collateralisation of territories is routinely used by the Hollywood majors. If a US studio acquires international distribution rights to a picture, it will typically seek to cross-collateralise profits and losses between territories, so that the producer of a film will only be entitled to a share of profits from a specific territory, once the combined profits of the film outweigh the combined losses.

However, the practice of cross-collateralising packages of pictures so that profits from one producer's picture are set against losses from those of another producer is regarded with suspicion in most quarters.

The producer may already have attracted some *equity investors* in the film. Such investors will be putting up money in return for a share of the profits, if any, from the completed film.[7] In such cases, pre-sales will be used to fund the shortfall between the equity finance already committed and the total budget. In other instances, it may be necessary to cover the whole budget from pre-sales. In the case of most European films aimed at an international audience, it is the willingness of these distributors to acquire the picture for distribution in their own territories which will determine whether the picture can be financed.

HOW THE SALES AGENT ASSESSES THE MARKETPLACE

Many of the top-flight sales agents are only prepared to go out and actively pitch a film if they are convinced that it will be produced and the major elements of the cast as well as the director are already in place.

The minimum guarantee for an individual film in a specific territory will be subject to negotiation between the sales agent and the distributor. But prior to initially approaching the distributors, the sales agent will usually have calculated a base value to be expected from major territories, based on elements including the budget of the film, the names of the director and the cast, and their track record at the box office in the territory concerned.

7 Film production is a high-risk industry and many pictures will fail to show a profit.

> **Many of the top-flight sales agents are only prepared to go out and actively pitch a film if they are convinced that it will be produced.**

Although the term "sales" has wide currency in the industry, in common usage it would be more accurate to say that the film is licenced, since rights for a country are assigned to a distributor for a certain period of years, usually 5 to 10. After that time the rights to the film revert to the owner of the negative. In the case of most independent films, the owner will be the producer or the sales agent who has an agreement to licence the film on behalf of the producer for a set number of years.

In some instances, the sales company itself will become a principal in the deal, so that it effectively agrees to bankroll the production from its own credit lines in return for certain rights. This means that the producer will not have to wait for a lengthy and complex series of pre-sale agreements to be negotiated worldwide. In such cases, the sales agent may be involved in the packaging of a feature, for example, by helping to find a director and casting it.

ASSESSING THE VALUE OF THE PACKAGE

In order to assess the likely value of the film in the marketplace, sales agents utilise a variety of research tools. Accessing this kind of information is frequently a time-consuming process since there is no single source of information for territories worldwide.

As part of this process, the sales agent will examine the theatrical grosses achieved by previous films from the director as well as analysing their performance on video in a specific territory. The sales agent also knows how much the distributor spent on marketing to achieve the gross together with the number of prints that were sent out.

The sales agent must also determine the part played by the various elements in the package, that is, how much is coming from video and how much will come from the theatrical release.

Sales agents will assemble figures from trade papers (the four main international trade papers are Variety, Screen International, The Hollywood Reporter and Moving Pictures International; these are supplemented by other trades in different countries), national organisations and conversations with local distributors in an effort to obtain the most comprehensive information possible. Most sales companies build their own files documenting the performance of films in various media in the major territories – again, another specialised task for which independent producers would have insufficient time and insufficient resources to do effectively.

Many leading sales agents maintain a list of the top 100 stars and directors, and their relative popularity in various world markets, enabling them to make judgements about the value of specific individuals in a market. They will look at the elements in a picture and rate them on a sliding scale of value. In the case of most of the major territories, the attraction and value of the film is dependent on both director and cast. They may also monitor box-office performance in foreign markets using their own resources. The trade papers can be used for tracking box-office performance, as well as to identify generic trends in particular markets.[8] This enables sales agents to maintain daily awareness of what is performing well in the marketplace.

> **Personal contact between the sales agents and the distributors is a fundamental aspect of business.**

The work of the sales company is not over once the film is sold. The established sales companies have to look after an inventory of pictures, which builds up over time. A company may have as many as 300-400 films in its library and the pictures are turning over all the time. Even though the film may not have been shown theatrically for several years, sales companies will have to file *royalty reports* on the film, calculating payments due to talent, based on television screenings in numerous different countries around the world.

The sales agents will also constantly be analysing the performance of the various distributors in each territory, allowing them to assess the relative merits of each company in handling different types of film. Because the film industry is heavily dependent on personal contact, the departure of a key executive from a particular distributor may lead to a dramatic change in the fortunes of a company, since with the executive may go a set of relationships that cannot easily be replaced. As a consequence, close monitoring of personnel changes is also critical. Different sales executives within companies specialise in different geographic areas. Detailed knowledge of a specific territory is usually gathered by talking to local distributors and other industry executives.

The work of the international sales executive entails year-round liaison with the international community of distributors, maintaining contact via telephone, fax or by setting up overseas visits. The international sales community is a small one, in which the maintenance of personal contact between the sales agents and the

8 One strategic advantage that the US studios hold over independents is the sheer volume of resources at their disposal for analysing the international marketplace. At a European Film Finance and Marketing Seminar organised by the Media Business School in Madrid in June 1991, Guy East, chief executive of Majestic Films and Television International, described the market information available to independents as "very, very limited". He observed that Majestic uses its own in-house research team to monitor performance of films in theatrical and ancillary media, as well as monitoring professional and company changes in each market.

distributors is a fundamental aspect of business. For mainstream pictures, the value of the principal territories in terms of the percentage contribution to the overall budget made by pre-sales generally approximates to the following: Australasia 2-3%, France 6%, Germany and Austria 10%, Italy 8%, Japan 10-12%, Spain 4% and the UK 10%.

ANCILLARY MARKETS

As well as the value of the film in terms of its theatrical release, it is important to try to assess its likely financial worth in the *ancillary markets* of video and television. Advances against television and video rights are an important component of production finance for European films. From 1988 to 1990, in the four major European markets (France, Germany, Italy, Spain), production budgets were covered on average at 20% by theatrical revenues and at 80% by video, television and foreign sales.

Within the video market where feature films largely predominate, rental can yield on average some 25% of revenues to the producer, while a blockbuster with a strong theatrical launch can deliver as much as 50%. Sell-through video (where films account for no more than 30-40% of titles) represents an average of just 12.5% of additional revenues, as margins in that sector are small.

However, determining in advance the potential video revenue for a film in a specific territory is not a straightforward task, as it depends on the video market of the country concerned and on the type of film (small, medium or big budget). Information on the performance of a film on video is not easy to obtain.

With television sales, some 75-80% of the sales price will go to the sales agent, with the distributor retaining the remainder. The sums remitted to the sales agent from these ancillary markets will be deducted from the minimum guarantee which the distributor has agreed to pay.

The practice of *sub-distribution*, under which the sales agent will appoint a local company in a specific territory to handle certain ancillary sales such as video or television, can be detrimental to the producer's interests. Such sub-distributors will themselves take a distribution fee, so that the producer is obliged to pay twice over in order to secure a sale.

ARRANGING THE FINANCE

Once a distributor has agreed to buy a picture from the sales agent or producer on the basis of the materials and subsequent discussions, a standard contract will be drawn up between the sales company and the distributor, containing an undertaking by the

Release windows in EC countries

	VIDEO	TELEVISION
Belgium	Informal agreements used for Flemish-speaking region French regulations used for French-speaking region	
Denmark	6 Months 1 Year for Local Films	18 Months
France	1 Year	1 Year for Pay-TV 2 Years for Free-TV
Germany	6 Months	18 Months for Pay-TV 2 Years for Free-TV
Greece	6-12 Months	30 Months
Ireland	6-12 Months	12-18 Months for Pay-TV 2-3 Years for Free-TV
Italy	9 Months	15 Months for Pay-TV 2 Years for Free TV
Luxembourg	Informal agreements used	
Netherlands	6 Months	18 Months for Pay-TV 2 Years for Free-TV
Portugal	1 Year	2 Years
Spain	6-8 Months	6-12 Months
UK	6 Months for Rental 1 Year for Sell-Through	1 Year for Pay-TV 2 Years for Free-TV

source : Espace Video Européen / authors' research

The windows (the delay between theatrical release and release in ancillary markets) are often based on informal agreements between sales agents, distributors and exhibitors, but they can also be set by national film bodies or the government. Therefore the windows above are subject to modification.

distributor to advance the majority of the minimum guarantee on *delivery* of the film, although a percentage may be paid when the contract is signed and when the film is in production. The term delivery has numerous definitions, but usually means the supply of a completed film – that is, a married print with front and end credits.

This agreement will usually include a **letter of credit** from the distributor's bank, in which it undertakes to advance the distributor the amount of the minimum guarantee at the required periods. As a payment for their services, sales agents will take a commission, usually between 10-20%, on the sale made.

These contracts, which usually amount to about 15-20 different agreements, are taken to one of a handful of banks which specialise in this kind of financing and, provided they are deals with reputable companies, the bank will lend the producer the money to cover the costs of production. This practice is known as **discounting** pre-sale contracts. The bank will often require pre-sale contracts. The credit-worthiness of the distributor is clearly a key element in this process, and the banks keep a close eye on the financial health of the various distributors around the world in an attempt to ensure that they are able to meet their commitments to pay for the film on delivery.

The bank will charge interest on the money (typically 2-3% above prime rates) as well as arrangement and management fees which, since film production is a high-risk business, may sometimes outweigh the interest charges.

THE COMPLETION GUARANTEE

A crucial element of this package will be the *completion guarantee*. There are certain companies which specialise in issuing completion guarantees, which are a form of insurance for the financiers of a film, designed to protect them in the event of the film running over budget. The guarantor provides a bond – essentially cash – guaranteeing that the film will be delivered on time, on budget and to the distributor's requirements. Should the film exceed its production costs, the guarantor is liable for the additional costs of the picture.

The guarantor charges the producer a fee in return for providing this security. Although there is no fixed rate – the structure of every bond is different and lower percentages are charged on high-budget films – up-front fees have tended to be in the 1.5% to 2% range, against an average of 6% ten years ago. Moreover, many producers have been seeking to exclude fixed costs – such as those for the script and director – from the budgetary total.

STRATEGIES FOR MARKETING TO THE SALES AGENT

It is the task of the producer to persuade the sales company to represent the film for international sales. This will very often be the first act of marketing to be carried out during the course of the film making process, and it is crucial for producers to make their film stand out from the competition since there is always a large number of competing producers, all with their own projects, and relatively few sales agents – particularly of the kind that can put up money to back a marketing campaign to sell a film.

Just as the process of marketing a film to audiences has firmly established ground rules, so the task of *pitching* the project to a sales agent has certain guidelines, which, if followed, give the producer a much greater chance of success.

This initial act of marketing to the sales agent is just as critical as the eventual marketing of the film to the public since, in many cases, without a sales agent it could be very difficult to get the finance together to start the production. Producers who start without the necessary funds or cash-flow are in an unfavourable position when seeking the last element of the financing,

> **" This initial act of marketing to the sales agent is just as critical as the eventual marketing of the film to the public. "**

and in such cases often lose valuable sales or distribution rights.

Many European films may not be suitable for an international sales agent to handle at this stage, because of considerations of language or subject matter. This does not mean that they will not be produced, but rather that the finance is more likely to come from other sources such as a national support system or a broadcaster. In such cases, the ground rules for pitching the project will be broadly similar to those outlined below.

ASSEMBLING THE PACKAGE

The first task for the independent producer is to excite the sales agent about the picture for which finance is being sought. If the sales company is sufficiently excited by the script and the elements of the film which are already attached (such as the director

> **The best-known film industry platitude is that "nobody knows anything", particularly when it comes to predicting which films will succeed at the box office.**

and potential cast) it may agree to represent the picture for foreign sales, thereby greatly enhancing the chances of the project finding the necessary financing.

Although the best-known film industry platitude is that "nobody knows anything", particularly when it comes to predicting which films will succeed at the box office, inside the industry there tends to be a consensus about exactly what kind of projects can be pre-sold. This is no guarantee that such films will go on to reap vast sums at the box office, but it does make it imperative that producers approaching industry sales agents should have done their homework, and arrive with projects which have clearly defined pre-sale potential.

MAKING THE APPROACH

Cold selling of any product is always difficult; for a feature film it is virtually impossible. The sales agents invariably have relationships with key producers, which guarantees them a certain number of films per year to sell. They will be very cautious about working with people with whom they have no prior relationship, unless those people come with a strong personal recommendation from someone whose judgement they implicitly trust.

For the sales agent, the risk inherent in taking on projects from people whom they do not know is simply too great to justify the time and expense involved.

As well as the expenditure involved, the sales company will be putting its own reputation on the line with the projects that it backs. Taking on just a handful of projects which the company is unable to sell to foreign distributors could have a serious impact on the company's reputation, since the world of international sales is a

> **Cold selling of any product is always difficult; for a feature film it is virtually impossible.**

small, close-knit community. It is by no means impossible for the nascent producer to gain an entrée, but as with all communities of this sort, a personal introduction will invariably help open doors.

Ideally, the producer should have the backing of a respected film/TV agent, who will take a commission should the project subsequently go into production. At the very least, the submission of the script should be preceded by an introductory telephone call made by an industry figure, known both to the sales agent and to the producer. Such an individual approach can help seduce the sales agent. "I like to think I'm being approached individually," says Mike Ryan of J&M Entertainment. "If I think everyone else is reading a script, I'm put off."

Reputable sales agents selling feature films have a finite amount of time for the task. Every feature film has a shelf life and a sell-by date. As a business, the sales agent's criteria for selecting its 6 to 12 projects a year often come down to the potential sales revenue of the project, the type of project (does it enhance the company itself, for example?) and the key elements of the project – director, cast, producer, script.

> " Reputable sales agents selling feature films have a finite amount of time for the task. Every feature film has a shelf life and a sell-by date. "

However, some sales agents will sometimes consider unsolicited scripts – they are not gripped by the same paranoia which has invaded the Hollywood studios, which simply return unsolicited scripts to the sender without opening them for fear that if they even glance at them they may later be sued for stealing an idea. The chances of an unsolicited script receiving a detailed examination from a European sales agent are not, particularly good.

CRUCIAL INGREDIENTS

To excite the interest of the sales agent, the producer, regardless of the language in which the film is to be made, must provide a package containing some basic ingredients. For most of the established sales agents the package must include the following:

- ### A SCRIPT
  This should embody an original and commercially accessible story. When submitted the script should be accompanied by a two- to three-page *synopsis* and an outline financing plan, which breaks down the budget of the film and provides a provisional outline of how the proposed costs of the project will be covered. Where possible, a summary of the main characters with the names of the actors and actresses being considered for the roles should also be provided.

- ### A DIRECTOR
  Preferably they should have an established track record.

- ### IDEALLY, ONE OR TWO WELL-KNOWN STARS
  A brief filmography of the principal confirmed members of the cast and crew can also be very helpful. If the producer has a track record, details of this will be advantageous.

The credibility of a project can also be boosted if the producer and the director have worked together on a film which achieved some level of success with the public. "The producer is very important," says Philippe de Chaisemartin, vice president, international sales, for French mini-major Gaumont. "If, for example, a prominent director like Maurice Pialat is in a package to be produced by Daniel Toscan du Plantier, who has worked with him before, it will be much easier to pre-sell than if the producer has no previous experience with that director."

In many instances, the attachment of an established *executive producer* will substantially boost the chances of the film being taken on by a sales agent. If the film is a non-English-language production, and it is being presented to a sales agent outside the country of origin, it should be presented in a high-quality English translation as well as in its original language.

The more of these elements that are combined in a single package, the stronger the chance that the film will interest, and subsequently be acquired by, a sales agent. Interest is the first step towards involving a sales agent in the financing of a film, but converting this interest into a financial commitment is the producer's main task at this stage of the film making process. A project won't survive on interest alone.

In Europe an established director with a track record for making bankable pictures can sometimes be as important as the cast in attracting finance for a picture. Directors such as Bernardo Bertolucci or Pedro Almodovar have clearly defined *arthouse* audiences in Europe and US (the term arthouse often being applied to non-English-language films which appeal to a mature audience often from upper socio-economic groups), which effectively guarantees a certain level of box-office receipts for films they direct. Some companies specialise in projects with "name" directors; CiBy Sales, a subsidiary of CiBy 2000, tends to handle pictures from specific directors operating within a defined style, such as Pedro Almodovar, Jane Campion and David Lynch. Films which are heavily dependent on first-time talent will also only be taken on in exceptional circumstances.

> **A project won't survive on interest alone.**

Indeed, in the arthouse sector, few films are pre-sold except on the basis of the director's name. Cast names are rarely considered important, and then only in relation to one or two key territories where a particular individual may be well known.

In some instances, the film has a better chance of being picked up by the sales agent if the generic elements of the picture (e.g. comedy, thriller or period drama) are clearly identifiable. "If the genre of the film is clear this helps prepare the ground to sell the film," says Adriana Chiesa, president of Adriana Chiesa Enterprises, the Italian sales company.

A point repeatedly stressed by European sales agents is that they frequently receive packages presented in an unprofessional manner. Documents are presented in a scruffy form, are poorly photocopied and contain many spelling mistakes. Since competition among aspiring producers is intense – many sales agents receive 600-700 scripts a year – packages submitted in such a form will not even secure tentative interest from sales agents.

Given the crucial importance of the script in attracting the interest of the sales agent, it is imperative that it, and the accompanying documents, should be neatly bound and covered. Visual images of the proposed film are considered helpful by some sales agents. The overall package should be attractive without being ostentatious, with the highest levels of professional presentation.

Providing the right tools to the sales agent is also critical from the viewpoint of selling the picture.

PREPARING TO SELL ENGLISH-LANGUAGE FILMS

Many sales agents construct their sales strategy for a picture around one of the three annual film markets.[9] In the case of the major sales agents, they will usually tie up the major territories on a film well in advance of one of these events, using the market to mop up smaller countries, and to gather market intelligence from distributors in key territories. For the smaller sales agents, the markets will be more of a focal point for their selling efforts. For all types of sales agent, the markets will also be a forum for discussing forthcoming projects.

The three key markets are the one held in Cannes in mid-May during the same period as the film festival, the Mercato Internazionale Film e Documentario (MIFED) held in Milan in late October, and the American Film Market (AFM) held in Los Angeles in late February. A smaller market, chiefly used by vendors of arthouse films, is held in Berlin in mid-February.

9 The different ways in which these markets are used is complex and is dealt with in Section Four: Markets and Festivals.

Whether the sales strategy for a film hinges on a market or not, certain basic tenets for initially creating distributor interest must be set in motion well before any market. Once again, the need to allow sufficient time for this process is paramount.

CREATING DISTRIBUTOR INTEREST

As has been emphasised above, the international sales industry is relatively small, and personal relationships carry considerable weight. As a result, a sales agent may have mentioned specific upcoming projects to the distributor, long before the film is ready to be sold. This will ease the way for the distributor when it comes to the process of actually selling the film. Because each film is a singular event – and any film, in theory at least, has the potential to be a hit – distributors are always eager to learn about new titles and there can be intense competition for certain titles.

Creating the right marketing strategy to excite distributors is crucial because of the quality of competition in the marketplace. In an increasing number of instances, European films may be competing for attention with films produced by the US majors. This is because the studios sometimes choose to retain only US distribution rights to their films and sell off the foreign rights to the film through an international sales agent. In such

> " Creating the right marketing strategy to excite distributors is crucial because of the quality of competition in the marketplace. "

cases the studios are able to utilise the sales agent's expertise in assessing the different strengths of each international market. Off-loading foreign rights to these companies is often the most effective way of maximising revenues while also reducing the studio's exposure to production costs.

In order to create such a "hot" title, the package presented to buyers should have the right ingredients in terms of script, director and talent. But just as the method of presentation counts for a great deal when a producer is pitching a project to a sales agent, the same applies when a sales company is approaching an international distributor in order to sell the film.

WHEN A SYNOPSIS WILL DO

The initial goal is to supply the distributor with the basic facts about the film which is to be sold. This will usually include a synopsis of the storyline or a full script, with information about the track record of the key persons involved, usually the director, cast, producer and, to a lesser degree, the screenwriter. Again, if the film to be shot is a non-English-language production, an English version of these materials will also need to be prepared. Some sales agents prefer to speak to distributors prior to sending out the synopsis, in an attempt to communicate some of the distinctive flavour of the film and whip up the distributors' interest in hearing more about the project, so that they will ask to read the script. According to Wendy Palmer, chief executive officer of CiBy Sales, the ideal length for such a synopsis is about "one page in length – it shouldn't be too long or it won't convey the excitement of the project". In some cases, the sales agent will use an outside writer such as a journalist to construct the synopsis.

Initially the sales agent will contact between two and six distributors in each territory, usually by telephone, before sending a written package, to assess their interest in the project. If there is an in-depth conversation on the telephone, the sales agent will usually give the distributor some idea of the price of the project at this stage. For arthouse pictures, the number of potential distributors will be much lower. However, as most sales agents will be having conversations with distributors all the time, often about matters related to earlier pictures they have released, the process of informing them about upcoming product doesn't necessarily follow a structured route.

Just as some sales agents prefer to feel that they are the only people reading a script submitted by a producer, many distributors like to feel they are being offered a picture on an exclusive basis. Auctioning pictures to the highest bidder is not always the most effective way to secure the right distribution for a project, although there are risks involved if a sales agent does not offer the project to competing companies.

> **" Each sales agent will usually have strong relationships with a particular set of distributors in the major territories. These will usually consist of distributors who specialise in the particular type of picture handled by that sales agent. "**

Each sales agent will usually have strong relationships with a particular set of distributors in the major territories. These will usually consist of distributors who specialise in the particular type of picture handled by that sales agent – such as, for example, low-budget action pictures, quality mainstream pictures featuring at least one well-known star, or specialist arthouse pictures.

The branding of certain distributors in terms of the pictures they handle will be an important element in attracting new projects from sales companies, and can often be a highly effective means of helping a distributor to carve out a distinct identity in an extremely competitive market.

In certain very rare cases, such as Little Buddha (directed by Bernardo Bertolucci, produced by Jeremy Thomas and sold by CiBy 2000), the project can be sold to distributors simply as a synopsis with a director and producer attached. In effect, the distributor is being asked to buy the film on the basis of track record and an instinctive feel for the idea. However, only a handful of European names are strong enough to allow a picture to be packaged so sparsely. In the case of Little Buddha, although the previous film from the Bertolucci/Thomas pairing – The Sheltering Sky – had performed below expectation at the box office, the project could be sold in this way because of its similarity to their film The Last Emperor, which won nine Oscars.

Some companies will not send out a synopsis, preferring to start with the full-length screenplay which is sent to selected buyers in the major territories, although increasingly the sales agent may also send out screenplays to smaller territories such as Argentina and Mexico. The script will usually be accompanied by details of the US distribution deal, which, if in place, should increase the value of the film. If a budget for the film has been drawn up, some financial details will also be released.

The job of the international distributor or the acquisition executive, is to acquire the next hit movie. If sales agents handle 6 to 12 pictures a year, distributors handle anywhere between 12 and 25 a year (see Section Five: Film Distribution in Europe). Therefore, in order to stay ahead of the competition, their task is to seek out at the earliest possible stage, any title that could be a potential acquisition. Thus *tracking* is the lifeblood of a distribution company, as without a new supply of film (or product) it would have no commodity with which to trade.

THE IMPORTANCE OF THE US DEAL

On some English-language films, securing a US deal will be a critical element in ensuring that there is a reasonable chance of raising funds for a film. As the US is the largest homogenous marketplace in the world, selling rights in that territory will enormously enhance the earning potential of a picture. Well-connected producers may be left to approach US sources themselves, otherwise it is the sales agents who will handle those negotiations.

For the other potential foreign buyers of a film, information about the US deal is important because it indicates the level of exposure that the film should receive. Of all global markets, by virtue of its size, the US market

" A US distribution deal is a valuable vote of confidence in the project. " "

ensures that most films receive some visibility through the media when they are released. If a film is a success in the US, other distributors will hope that that success will create a buzz which will percolate through to other countries.

The fact that a film has a US distribution deal is a valuable vote of confidence in the project, since it is made by buyers in the world's most important – and probably most lucrative – market.

This assumes, of course, that the film is released in the US before most other territories and that it is well received there. In cases where a film performs poorly in the US, the foreign distributor may experience the negative effects of high visibility, since bad publicity may well travel in advance of the film and deter customers in other territories.

A US deal can also confer credibility on a film, particularly in cases where the picture involves relatively unknown talent. Such distribution deals may be struck with a major but in the case of most European films they are likely to be secured with independent distributors.[10]

For non-English-language films, securing a US deal can be much more difficult than for English-language pictures, as distributors perceive that such films will have a difficult time securing adequate returns in the US market. Moreover, since the Americans subtitle rather than dub their non-English-language films, the performance of these pictures in ancillary markets is less predictable, a factor which will often make distributors more reluctant to acquire these pictures.

STRATEGIES FOR PRE-SELLING NON-ENGLISH-LANGUAGE PICTURES

Non-English-language pictures are usually sold once they have been completed. The international markets are dominated by English-language films (overwhelmingly of US origin) and hence

---

10 Such independent distributors would include Fine Line, Miramax (acquired by Walt Disney in April 1993, although it still operates under its own name), Samuel Goldwyn and Sony Classics (which is owned by Japan's Sony Corporation, but which specialises in independent pictures).

very few buyers – outside the home territory in which the film was produced – are willing to risk buying such films without seeing some footage.

Non-English-language films tend to be handled by sales agents based in the country from which the film originated. However, some sales companies argue that if a producer has a non-English-language project with the potential to do significant business in areas outside its home territory, the picture may benefit if it is handled by an English-language sales company with expertise in selling major pictures.

Some non-English-language films can be pre-sold in the major territories, usually if they come with a name director. But for a relatively unknown director, unless there is strong casting in place, such a picture will be very difficult to pre-sell. A first film is almost impossible to pre-sell. Even with a second film from a director who achieved success with a first picture, the script will be just as important in attracting pre-sales.

Productions originating in the smaller countries, such as Scandinavia or Benelux, will invariably also be difficult to pre-sell. Even when the completed film is sold, it will usually be done on the name of the director rather than the stars, since there is a severe shortage of European stars who can attract audiences across the continent. However, overseas interest in the film may be much greater if the film becomes a hit in its home territory, or if it receives international recognition – for example, a Best Foreign Film Oscar nomination for the Belgian film Daens helped with its international sales.

Bill Stephens, Film Four International director of sales, says that in the case of most of the specialised films which he handles, the only marketing that he would do prior to a film's completion would be to produce a sales flyer for the film before it goes into production. The flyer would have the synopsis, principal cast and crew list, the first image or title style of the film, and possibly a brief filmography of the director and leading members of the cast. The full-scale advertising and marketing campaign for the film will usually only start once the picture is completed and, in some cases, if the film is entered in a festival.

An exception to this would be a film featuring a major European director, where it can be extremely helpful to keep the distributor informed throughout the shoot.

For example, in the case of The Best Intentions, handled by Film Four International, Bill Stephens initially informed distributors by post of plans for a project written by Ingmar Bergman, to be co-produced by a group of European broadcasters.

Subsequently, he sent the script to the top distributors in Europe. They were also provided with a monthly newsletter updating them on the progress of the shoot and sent a photo album providing them with shots from the set. This process of continual communication with the distributors was designed to ensure that they had a high level of awareness of the film when the film was completed and the sales pitch was made. Later, certain distributors flew to Sweden to see the television version of the film or to view selected footage from the feature version. Most of the sales on the picture were completed by this stage.

The film was later accepted for the official competition at the Cannes Film Festival, which helped seal sales agreements with the last few distributors. Stephens' strategy for this picture throughout was to constantly inform distributors of the high-quality pedigree and production values of the film.

Even in the most successful cases, overall sales on a non-English-language film will only represent a very small contribution to the budget. "Three years ago it used to be possible to get 30% of the budget in sales. Now you can only achieve 10% of the budget this way," says Alexandre Heylen, managing director of Mainstream Films, which handled Toto le Héros. The fall is partly due to the sharp increase in the cost of prints and advertising for a film, which makes distributors far more unwilling to take a risk on a film they have not seen. The majority of funds will come from equity investment, tax-incentive schemes or via the subsidy system. Other non-English-language pictures may have to rely for their financing on a pre-sale to a local broadcaster or on co-productions with one or two other countries in Europe.

> **The major thrust in selling a picture will be made at the key international film markets.**

An alternative strategy for a small number of selected projects outside the mainstream with a strong director, script and perhaps one star, is to approach distributors to put equity into a picture in return for certain distribution rights.

In such cases, since the distributors are actually putting up cash on an equity basis, they will have much greater involvement in the production of the film than if they simply acquire it on a pre-sale basis. They will of course be able to demand a voice in the casting of the project, are likely to be involved in the budgeting of the film and will be able to influence the marketing campaign from an early stage. If the distributors feel they have a voice in the production process they may be much more willing to take a risk on buying the project before it goes into production.

KEY POINTS

TIME
- **Allow sufficient time**
  Although it may seem routine, having sufficient time to plan and execute every element in the marketing of the film is crucial in creating a successful campaign.

CONTACTS
- **Utilise contacts and try to find experienced partners**
  Personal introductions to the sales agents will help enormously in persuading them to consider a project, since few sales agents are willing to contemplate films from people who approach them cold. Ideally, at least some of the personnel involved with the film should have a track record.

PACKAGE ELEMENTS
- **Ensure the right elements are included in the package**
  The package presented to the sales agent should include:

  - a script
  - name of director
  - potential cast
  - outline financing plan
  - filmographies of cast and crew can also be helpful. It may also help if the generic elements of the film (e.g. comedy, action thriller etc) are presented so the project has a strong marketing hook.

DOCUMENT PRESENTATION
- **Professional presentation of documents is vital**
  Badly typed documents full of spelling mistakes stand no chance of consideration. The package must stand out from the competition.

SALES AGENT
- **The sales agent should participate in the risk**
  If sales agents do not offer minimum guarantees or put up money towards the marketing costs, then producers must feel confident that the agent will be motivated to make sales even though the agent is not taking any of the risks.

But the major thrust in selling a picture will be made at the key international film markets and, to a lesser extent, festivals, which are held on an annual basis and are key dates in the diaries of many film executives. The next section will examine the most effective way of preparing for these events, and analyse how best to exploit the opportunities they present.

MARKETS AND FESTIVALS

" The atmosphere is similar to that of a bazaar, in which hundreds of films are bought and sold within the space of a few days. "

The major markets and festivals are a crucial date in the diaries of film sales and marketing executives. A different strategy will be devised for each market or festival. In broad terms, the most important factor determining the approach to a specific event will be whether it is a market or a festival, since the two events are quite different in nature.

As discussed in the previous section, International Sales, the three most important film markets are Cannes in mid-May during the same period as the film festival, MIFED held in Milan in late October, and the American Film Market (AFM) held in Los Angeles in late February. A smaller market, held in mid-February during the Berlin Film Festival, is primarily used for sales of art-house films (see chart of major events in the film calendar, p.72/3). At the three markets, most of the major international sales agents will hire office space from where they will conduct business with one of the hundreds of film distributors who are there to buy films. The atmosphere is similar to that of a bazaar, in which hundreds of films are bought and sold within the space of a few days.

Few of the festivals, with the exception of Cannes and Berlin, incorporate an official film market. The primary aim of a festival is to showcase films for the benefit of the press and the public. Many distributors, however, will often attend selected festivals to see films which they are considering buying and to talk to any visiting sales agents and producers.

To maximise the value that can be obtained from the markets it is imperative that sales companies plan their campaigns for each market well in advance and prepare certain key materials, which will be used to attract the attention of the distributors, the trade press and in the case of Cannes, the consumer press. As is stressed throughout this book, allocating the required time and resources to planning and executing all aspects of the marketing campaign is a critical, but often under-valued, means of helping to ensure success.

This section will examine the strategies and tools to be used under different circumstances, and will also demonstrate how producers can maximise the value of such events.

WORKING THE MARKETS

The larger sales agents will tend to use the markets for informing distributors of what is in the pipeline and updating their knowledge of trends in the key territories. Although the sales agents will maintain constant contact with international distributors throughout the year, the markets present an opportunity to meet face-to-face with a large number of people in a relatively short space of time.

If a large sales agent is pre-selling a picture, most of the deals for the larger territories will often have been completed by the time the company arrives at the market. The sales agent will use the market to try to mop up sales on unsold territories, which are usually the smaller territories which are difficult to pre-sell.

For the smaller companies, the markets are used for more of a sales push, since the ingredients of the specialised films which they tend to handle are often not strong enough to be pre-sold on the basis of telephone conversations and mailing of the script. Instead, they will need to have face-to-face conversations with the potential buyers of the pictures and will often screen the completed film in an effort to incite interest.

When sales agents first acquire the rights to sell a particular picture, they will analyse how the proposed schedule for the pre-production, production and post-production of the film ties in with the schedules of the various film markets (see appendix Lifestages of a Film). They will then draw up a strategy for approaching each event, with the goal of building a momentum or *buzz* around a picture, which will be timed to peak when the picture is first screened at a market. The nature of this strategy will be a crucial means of boosting sales.

THE FIRST MARKET

At this first market, the aim of the sales agent will usually be to generate an initial sense of excitement around the project, based on certain elements in the film such as the likely cast, the director or the storyline. This will form the prelude to a full-blooded sales campaign which is likely to start at the second market.

Even before the market opens, the sales agents will talk to distributors about forthcoming films as part of their regular dialogue with international buyers, so that the distributors arrive at the market with some prior knowledge of the project.

KEY MARKETING TOOLS AT THE FIRST MARKET

The marketing tools used during the first market will continue to be used at subsequent markets, but they will usually be augmented by other materials. The main elements are as follows:

- **Shooting Script**

  The shooting script is often the element in the package which is most likely to hook potential buyers. Most distributors will wish to see this script, particularly if they are being asked to put up relatively large sums of money for the picture. Alternatively, distributors may wish to take the script away and read it on their return home, enabling them to make a considered decision about a picture. If possible, scripts should be sent out to key buyers six to eight weeks before a market, to allow distributors sufficient time to read them. This makes the market meetings more effective, since the sales agent will be dealing with distributors who have read the script and who will base their offer accordingly.

  > **"Scripts should be sent out to key buyers six to eight weeks before a market."**

- **The Synopsis**

  Both a short and a long synopsis of the film will be useful for buyers who are at a market for just a few days and who therefore do not have time to read entire scripts. Also, full scripts won't always be available for markets, so being armed with a synopsis in such a case would be essential. Since many hundreds of films will be on offer at each market, the sales agent must have planned an effective campaign for attracting buyers and for maintaining their interest in a project. Bearing this in mind, the synopsis is an essential marketing tool.

- **Stills, Filmographies and Background Information**

  Filmographies and biographical information on the leading members of cast and crew can be very effective tools in helping the sales effort, but too often they are neglected. Such neglect may damage the chances of success of the film. Such information will help the buyer to evaluate the project based on the calibre, pedigree and previous box-office results of the key actors, the director and other personnel. This material can be supplied either by the production company or by the agent representing the individual concerned. It may be supported by colour or black-and-white stills of the cast – especially in the case of new talent – as this will help the distributor to visualise the film or screen characters.

- ## Publicity and Press

Publicity will play a crucial role in informing the industry and press about a film when it is first launched at a market.

It will be handled either by the sales agent's in-house marketing person, or by an outside publicity company. In the major territories, there are companies which specialise in film publicity. Such companies will usually be hired by the producer, who will make decisions in conjunction with the sales agent. If there is no sales agent or publicity company attached, the responsibility for press and publicity would then fall to the producer.

The first task of the publicity company will be to ensure that the industry is aware that a film is going to happen. This will be achieved by issuing a press release on the film, which will include details of the director and key cast members together with a brief summary of the storyline. This is often done by the **unit publicist**, an individual attached to the shoot to handle press and publicity. For larger pictures, information about the US distribution deal (if any) may also be included. If this occurs at the same time as a market, then a more detailed release will be circulated to all trade press attending the market for inclusion in their daily publication. The unit publicist's goal will be to maximise media coverage of the film, both to make the public aware of the film at an early stage and also to interest potential distributors.

In addition to issuing a press release, the publicist will often organise a press conference, at which the trade and selected consumer press will be invited to meet and question the stars and director of the film. The goal is to generate early press coverage which will help to interest distributors in the film.

Such press conferences are a particular feature of Cannes, where a huge number of representatives of both consumer and trade press from around the world are gathered. Although much of their attention is focused on the completed films showing at the festival, the mere presence of so many journalists and photographers can offer ample scope for the sales agent to secure coverage of films which are at the earliest stage of development.[1]

At the American Film Market and MIFED, the press presence is largely confined to journalists from the trade publications, because these two markets are not accompanied by a festival where completed films are shown in competition with each other. At the AFM, distributors will occasionally host celebrity receptions to help launch a film, but at MIFED there are very few press events.

1 The number of accredited press at Cannes is generally about 3500, but it is estimated that this number may be doubled by numbers of unaccredited individuals. These figures can include as many as 50 or 60 television crews.

- **Announcing Ad**

  The announcing ad will often be used to complement the press release at the first market and will be placed in one of the film trade magazines.

  The four main international trade papers are Variety, Screen International, The Hollywood Reporter and Moving Pictures International.[2] They are supplemented by other publications such as le Film Français, the French trade publication, Film Echo in Germany and Cinema d'Oggi in Italy, as well as a number of other trades in different countries.

  During the three main film markets, some or all of these publications publish daily editions, which are just circulated at the film market itself and which sales agents frequently use to advertise their films.

- **Trade Listings**

  Once a film has been unveiled, a sales agent will include it in the trade listings published by the film trade publications in their bumper issues, which appear in advance of each market. Trade listings comprise a comprehensive list of the sales agents who will be attending a particular market, together with brief details of the films they will be selling at the market. The listings will offer an alphabetical guide to the sales agents present.

  > **The value of free publicity, such as trade listings, is often under-estimated.**

  The value of free publicity, such as trade listings, is often under-estimated. At Cannes, for example, there is no official guide to all the films on offer at the market so the trade papers offer the distributor invaluable information about what's being sold at the market. Bumper issues will also be widely consulted at both MIFED and AFM, although official information about the films being offered for sale is more readily available at these two markets.

  Production listings of those films currently in production (or post-production) also appear in most weekly trade publications. These are used by buyers to track the films in which they may be interested.

---

2 Variety and The Hollywood Reporter publish daily editions in Los Angeles, Monday to Friday. Variety also publishes a separate international weekly edition, and The Hollywood Reporter's Tuesday edition carries an international section, both of which are circulated around the world. Screen International and Moving Pictures International are both published in the UK on a weekly basis, and are circulated to subscribers around the world.

KEEPING IN TOUCH

From the first to the second market, the distributor must maintain constant communication with potential buyers of the film, as sometimes it may take two or three markets to convince buyers to put up money for the film. In the case of non-English-language films, it will be difficult to achieve international sales until the project is finished, so the sales agent must maintain constant contact with the distributor from the moment the picture is unveiled until completion. This may involve using the trade press again, for example by issuing a press release and placing advertisements that announce the start or end of principal photography.

The publicity company or sales agent will usually attach a unit publicist to the production once the film starts shooting. The publicist will seek to generate location reports in mainstream magazines and newspapers, as well as in the trade press, usually focusing on a certain aspect of the film, such as the name of a certain star or director, as a hook to interest the media. In other cases, topical or unusual subject matter may be used to incite press coverage.

Another technique is to have a closed set or confine entry to a few selected journalists, in the hope that this will generate an atmosphere of intrigue and heightened expectation among the public in the run-up to the film's release. This strategy will be particularly suited to films which involve unusual subject matter or which have a novel plot thrust. The goal in such cases is to focus the interest of the public on those elements which most sharply distinguish the film from the competition.

THE SECOND MARKET

At the second market, the sales agent will use an additional set of tools to market the picture to distributors, especially if some footage of the film is already available. However, some of the materials used at an earlier stage, such as the script, will be used again. It is at the second market that the sales campaign will usually start in earnest, although it will probably not peak until the film receives its market screening, which may not occur until the project has its third, or even fourth, market outing.

The first two or three days of this market will often be spent distributing material such as synopses and stills to the potential buyers, and setting up meetings for the third or fourth day of the market when the deals can be negotiated. As a result of those meetings, the sales agent will hope to receive a number of firm offers on the picture and if the sum offered is acceptable the deal will be closed.

KEY MARKETING TOOLS AT THE SECOND MARKET

- **Shooting Schedule**

  If the film is still shooting or in post-production, a production schedule will help distributors to determine the likely date when the film could be delivered. This in turn will help distributors to decide how the film might fit into their likely release schedule.

- **The Office Display**

  The office displays, featuring posters, stills and blow-ups from the film (if available), are crucial marketing tools at this stage, since film is a visual medium and these items will implant an image of the film in the minds of the potential distributors.

  The poster – which is also known as a **one-sheet**, or as the **key art** – will be based on those elements which the sales agent feels are the key selling points of the film. The most common format used for posters is 27in x 40in (707mm x 1000mm).

  At this stage the poster is often a simple blow-up of a photograph and title style. This is not necessarily the image that will be used in the final campaign for the film. It will usually comprise an enlarged still with a strong title style and credit block, which gives distributors a more concrete idea of the film and will also provide them with ideas about how they might sell the film to their public.

  In the UK there are a handful of companies that specialise in creating these posters for film companies. Elsewhere in Europe this work is usually undertaken by graphic design companies and those working on a freelance basis.

  The sales agent will commission the poster company to produce a design based on the key elements of the film. In many cases, the designer will be given as little as two weeks to prepare a poster for a market, sometimes for reasons beyond the control of the sales agent – for example, it can take time to get a director and cast actually to sign on the dotted line.

  If the sales agent doesn't commission the work within a reasonable time frame, there may be insufficient time to create an attractive image, and certain suppliers contracted by the poster company – the printers, for example – may have to be paid rush fees. As a result, costs will rise, while quality will suffer. When the sales agent comes to sell the project at a market they may rapidly discover that a poor poster results in a poor level of sales.

  It is vital, therefore, to allow enough time for the creation of an effective sales poster campaign, otherwise the film will be disadvantaged when competing with the enormous number of other pictures in the marketplace.

- **Stills**

  Stills are an important part of the office display and may also be packaged in books to be shown to visiting distributors. For films which have started production, such stills are a vital marketing tool as they are a highly effective means of conveying the visual style of a picture and highlighting key members of the cast. Since just two or three visual images of a film may be used repeatedly around the world to promote the film, everything needs to be done to ensure that the photographs are as effective as possible.

  It is vital, therefore, to ensure that a photographer is on set while the film is shooting. A photographer who is attached to a film throughout most or all of the shoot is known as the **unit photographer**, as these will often be people specialising in such work.

  Where budgets are lower, a freelance photographer should be hired for just a few days to cover the key scenes of the picture.

  Increasingly, many sales agents and producers hire photographic agencies to take stills – in countries such as France, for example, where the number of unit photographers has steadily declined. All photographers should be made to feel welcome on set and treated like a member of the crew, so that they have the best possible opportunities to take first-class photographs.

  In many cases, the director will see the carrying out of stills photography on set as an intrusion. It is therefore down to the producer to ensure that the unit photographer is allowed to do the job properly and that everyone is aware of the importance of the photographs. If this is not done, the marketing campaign for the film may be adversely affected and the performance of the film may therefore suffer once it is released.

  " Photographers should be made to feel welcome on set and treated like a member of the crew, so that they have the best possible opportunities to take first-class photographs. "

  In order to secure the best possible images of the cast, it may be necessary to set aside a day which is dedicated to photographs. Stills taken at the location or studio where the film is shooting are generally much more effective than any shots made of key cast members at a later stage, as they will usually feature the actors in character. It will also be cheaper to shoot at this point, since most of the cast are in one place. If a film doesn't feature well-known stars, it will be particularly important to create the stills while the film is shooting, since individual photographs of the stars taken later won't have much appeal to the media. In such cases, the role of the stills as a marketing tool will be to convey the film's mood rather than to sell the picture based on its leading actors.

Moreover, once a film is completed, it may be extremely difficult to persuade members of the cast to participate in photo shoots related to the film, since they will often have moved on to fulfil other commitments. The cost of shooting stills once the film is completed may be as much as five times higher than it would be while the film is in production.

In some cases it may be possible to secure photographic images of the location and members of the cast while the film is still in pre-production. These images can be used for the books of stills or as the basis for trade advertising. Tracy Payne, formerly sales director for Spain's Iberoamericana, used such an approach on the film Jamón Jamón, directed by Bigas Luna. "The production team went to the location at Los Monegros in advance of shooting," she says. "They sent a few photographs back and we were able to do a montage of a young girl with her back to the camera, which we used as the basis for an advertising campaign in the trade papers."

> " To secure the best possible images of the cast, it may be necessary to set aside a day which is dedicated to photographs. "

Sales companies will prepare books with as many as 50 stills. But in such cases it is vital that the stills are held back until the right moment, otherwise their publicity value will be wasted. For instance, some producers sell the stills to photographic agencies who will syndicate sales to magazines around the world. But the agencies will often fail to ensure that the stills appear at the most effective time for publicising a film. For instance, the agency may sell the photographs to a national magazine for publication six months before the film is released in that territory. As a consequence, when the film is about to be released the publication will refuse to publish the photographs again, and a major opportunity to publicise the film has been lost.

- **The Showreel**
  If some footage of the film has already been shot, the sales agent will often want to cut a showreel, which will usually be between 5 and 15 minutes in length. In effect, the showreel is a précis of the film, and as such offers a more comprehensive taste of the film than a trailer. Because the film may still be incomplete, a temporary music track will often be used to accompany the showreel, and the footage may be taken from a rough cut. The showreel may either be put together on film, in which case it is likely to cost between $14,600-21,900 (ECU13,100-19,650), or on video, $7300-11,680 (ECU6550-10,480). These are specialist tools and should be assembled by specialist companies with a knowledge of

what is required – cutting a showreel is very different from cutting a feature or even a trailer.

- ## Rough Cut of the Trailer
  The rough cut of a trailer for the film may also be shown to potential buyers. As well as giving distributors a sense of how the film will or can be marketed, the trailer will help reinforce the impact of the showreel by singling out particularly dramatic moments in the film, and imparting a sense of the overall tone of the film. Such a trailer may be as short as 30 seconds but in most cases it will last two to three minutes. If cut on high-quality videotape, it will usually cost around $4380 (ECU3930).

- ## The Brochure
  For some films, the sales company will create a brochure to promote the film to both distributors and press. However, brochures are costly, and consequently will only be used where judged to be particularly effective. Also, it can be difficult to obtain access to material which has been approved by leading members of the cast. Frequently, lengthy negotiations with the agents representing major talent may be necessary before they are willing to permit the use of certain photographs, as they will be concerned that the star in question is being given sufficient prominence in promotional materials.

  The cover of the brochure for the film will often be a version of the artwork used for the poster. The paper used for the cover will usually be of a heavier stock to lend weight and texture to the document. Inside, the brochure will usually contain a synopsis of the film, designed to arouse the interest of the buyer, together with information about the track record of the director and the principal cast and, in some cases, the producer. A selection of stills be will used to accompany the text. The overall length will depend on the budget of the film, but it will usually be anything from 8 to 32 pages in length.

  Some distributors choose to wait until after the film has been completed before they work on the brochure. In so doing, the brochure will reflect the final film (as opposed to producing one in the earlier stages when the nuances of the visual image are still being developed) and therefore will have a longer shelf life and be more cost-effective. On many non-English-language pictures, the sales agent may just rely on a flyer until the film is complete.

  For an event such as Cannes, as many as 1500-2000 such brochures will be created, each of which could have cost between $11,700-29,200 (ECU10,500-26,200), depending on the production values and use of colour. Such costs mean that, in most cases, it will be only larger films which will be able to afford such elaborate brochures.

Following the second market, the sales agent will maintain regular contact with the distributors so that they are appraised of all developments concerning the picture.

THE THIRD MARKET

By the time of the third or the fourth market, the film will usually be ready for screening in its entirety. At this stage in its life, it may also be entered for screening at a film festival.

KEY MARKETING TOOLS AT THE THIRD MARKET

- **Trade Advertising**
At this market the goal of trade advertising is to maximise the visibility of the picture. On larger pictures, to ensure that the film has a high profile, the sales companies will often take ***double-page spreads*** in which an advertisement is spread over two pages. These advertisements will usually be run in the bumper editions of the trades and in the daily market issues. This advertising may run over several days, culminating on the day the film is to receive its market screening.

One way of ensuring high visibility for a picture is to take a prime position such as a front or back cover or an early right-hand page in such publications. As the film is likely to be competing with hundreds of others for the attention of potential buyers, it is important to secure the best advertising possible, within the constraints of the marketing budget. Such prime positions will often need to be booked with the trade papers in advance of the market. Advertisement costs can range from $500 (ECU448) for a quarter-page black-and-white, to $6000 (ECU5400) for a full page in full colour. Premium positions usually cost up to 25% extra. Cost-effective marketing calls for rigorous negotiation with trade papers as advertising costs are one of the major cost centres in selling a film to the international distribution community.

However, in the case of pictures where the elements such as the story, cast or director have already proved strongly intriguing to distributors, it may be preferable to pursue a more low-key approach so that the promotional material for the film is targeted at a few selected buyers. In certain instances, it is possible to build an aura of exclusivity around the film by reducing the volume of advertising and concentrating on targeting individual buyers and on direct mail.

- ## The Market Screenings

Once the film is completed, the task of the sales agent handling an English-language film will be to complete sales on unsold territories, which will often include many of the smaller countries around the world.

For a company selling a non-English-language film, the completion of the film and its subsequent screening at the market will usually mark the start of the full-scale international sales campaign for the film, since it will have only been possible to have achieved very limited sales on the picture prior to the commencement of the market.

> **For a company selling a non-English-language film, the completion of the film and its subsequent screening at the market will usually mark the start of the full-scale international sales campaign for the film.**

The market screening acts as the showcase for the film. For the sales agent, the object of the market screening is to persuade distributors to buy the film at the highest possible price. The distributor wants to ensure that the completed film matches the expectations aroused by the script. On the basis of this screening, those distributors who have not yet committed to the film will make a decision as to whether to buy the film.

The market screening will be booked in advance by the sales agent, either through the market organisers or directly with an individual cinema. In the case of Cannes, the market screenings are held in the Palais des Festivals and in public cinemas located in the city itself which, for the duration of the event, are given over to the festival. At MIFED, the screenings will either be held in cinemas located inside the exhibition hall – the Fiera Internazionale di Milano – or at cinemas elsewhere in the city (see chart showing MIFED screening schedule p.66/67). At the AFM, the screenings will usually be held at one of the many cinema complexes in the host city, Los Angeles.

> **Ideally, the market screening should be held somewhere around the middle of the market, as this will allow the sales agent time to create a buzz prior to the screening.**

Ideally, the market screening should be held somewhere around the middle of the market, as this will allow the sales agent time to create a buzz prior to the screening. The time between the screening and the end of the market will then be used to close deals on the film with various distributors.

As with cost-effective and well-placed trade advertising, knowing when and where to screen a film at a market or festival – particularly for its first screening – requires a clear strategy. Buyers

Sample MIFED screening schedule

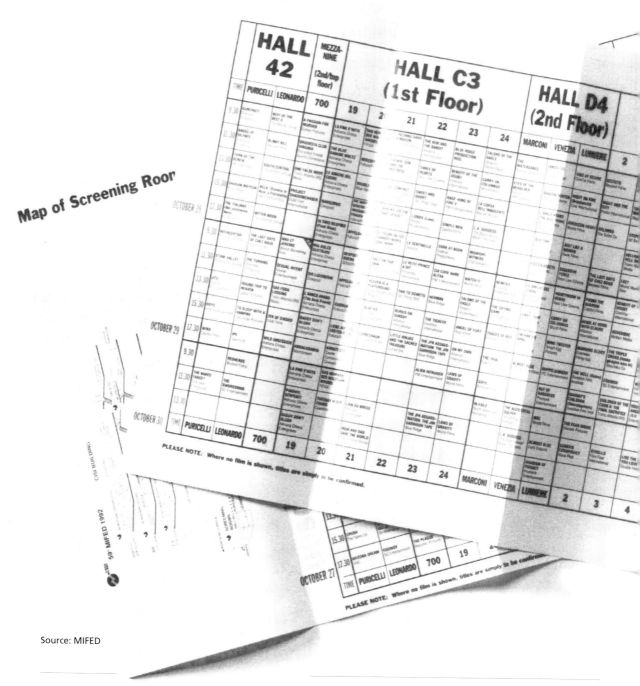

Source: MIFED

59th
MIFED
OCTOBER 25-30
1992
OFFICIAL
SCREENING
SCHEDULE

Late changes will be listed on the video wall (main reception) and on the video screens around the market, as well as on the noticeboard in the screenings office and outside each relevant screening room.

Telephone:
Screenings office   4303 6794/4303 6812
Dolby technical office   4997 7125
Dion Hanson
Main print storage   4997 7121

Prepared and
published by

together
with   MOVING PICTURES

will have been waiting since the early days of production to see the film, and with hundreds of films screening and perhaps thousands of dollars being spent on promoting and advertising, selecting the right day, the right time and the right cinema for the screening is of paramount importance. Only through close discussion with market/festival organisers, completion of a screening application on time and a thorough knowledge of how each market works, can this crucial step be successfully achieved.

In some cases, there will be more than one market screening of a picture, although the sales agent may limit the number of screenings of the film in the hope of creating a sense of exclusivity around the project. As the community of distributors is small, it should be possible to reach the most important buyers with one or two screenings. It is crucial to ensure that distributors are aware of the timing of each screening. Sales agents will use the daily trade papers at the market as their main vehicle for advertising screening times, although they will also seek personally to alert distributors. As competition for the attention of buyers is very strong, many sales agents provide screening schedules and personal tickets.

> " Selecting the right day, the right time and the right cinema for the screening is of paramount importance. "

Market screenings generally cost between $750-1000 (ECU672-900). If a cinema in a city centre is rented, particularly for an evening screening, the costs can rise to $2000-4000, but the film will benefit from a greater sense of exclusivity.

- **Press Books**
  These will include bringing together much of the material discussed above. The press kit will be aimed at both the consumer and the trade press and will be designed to maximise interest in the film. The press kit will usually include:

  - A synopsis of the film (1-2 pages).

  - Filmographies with previous credits of producer, director, screenwriter and the three or four leading members of the cast together with similar details on any distinguished member of the crew, for example, if a noted cinematographer is being used.

  - Production notes on the film itself.

  - Full list of cast, crew and technical information including running time.

In certain cases, large numbers of such press books will be required. For instance, at the Cannes Film Festival where a film is in the official competition, at least 2000 such press books, as well as at least three or four black-and-white stills from the film, are needed for those in attendance. In addition, a selection of 35mm colour transparencies for magazines will be supplied. The information has to be in English and French. The total costs of such a book will be anywhere from $5000-15,000(ECU4500-13,500).

The sales agent will also prepare some short clips from the film for use by television stations, as a means of boosting media coverage and so raising the profile of the film among the public.

MARKETING BUDGETS DURING SALES

The decision as to how much money to spend on selling on a film will be subject to constant modification as the picture goes through its lifestages (see appendix) and is presented to potential buyers. Much will depend on who is cashflowing the marketing costs and who will ultimately pay those same costs; the sales agent might put up the marketing money, but normally it is the producer of a given film who will eventually pay the costs of selling the title.

TIMING THE DEAL

The decision by a sales agent or distributor as to when to buy or sell a film will always depend on a calculated gamble, with different factors in play each time.

For the sales agent, determining the right moment to accept an offer from a distributor will involve a strong element of risk. The sales agent may receive an offer for a picture somewhere below the asking price set at the first market at which the film is being sold. In the case of a film which is being pre-sold, the sales agent must decide whether to accept the offer or whether to wait until some

CHECKLIST

The text below outlines the main costs incurred when selling a film. The ranges given are intentionally wide, as each film should have its own unique strategy and be budgeted according to its projected sales revenues.

RANGE
- $30,000 – 250,000

OVERHEADS OF TRAVELLING TO MARKET
- Travel, Car Rental, Taxis
- Hotel and Subsistence
- Office Hire, including Video Hire
- Local Staffing
- Special Receptions/Entertainment

SPECIFIC FILM COSTS
- Synopsis
- Stills and Colour, Special Stills, Book Sales Sheets/Brochures
- Design & Printing of Sales Sheets/Brochures
- Advertising: Space and Design
- Publicity
- Showreels
- Market Screenings/Special Screenings
- Shipping of Prints & Publicity
- Entertainment (e.g. Receptions for Special Screenings)
- Festival Costs (Subtitling, Press Attachés, Travel of Cast/Director)

footage of the film is available, in the hope of getting the asking price. A sales agent with absolute confidence in the project may be willing to wait until the film is completed. However, in other cases, the sales agent may be more inclined to accept an earlier offer, even if it does not quite match the asking price. At this early stage, the sales agent is selling a vision of the film, rather than a completed project. Once a film is screened, it will largely stand or fall on its own merits, and as a result it will be much harder to secure a good price for relatively indifferent material.

There is generally less room for manoeuvre in the case of non-English-language pictures, since as was explained in the last section, it is much harder to sell such pictures prior to footage

> **The decision by a sales agent or distributor as to when to buy or sell a film will always depend on a calculated gamble, with different factors in play each time.**

being available. So when the completed film is screened at a market, this will often be the first opportunity to assess the reaction of international distributors.

Equally, the distributor must decide when would be the best time to make an offer for a film – a bid on a film that is felt to be particularly strong may better be made at pre-sale stage rather than waiting until the picture is completed, when prices may rise.

Conversely for some films, particularly those in the $8-15 million budget range, sellers will be asking for a relatively high minimum guarantee, yet the buyer may feel that the ingredients of the package (stars, director and script) as laid out on paper, do not immediately justify the asking price. As a result, the distributor will insist on waiting to view the finished film.

There are also some territories, Scandinavia for example, where the relatively limited number of distributors means that there is little competition for pictures. As a result, such distributors can afford to be very selective in their approach to buying pictures and they will often wait to see the finished film before making a decision as to whether to acquire it. Buyers in other territories, for example Korea, tend to have very specific ideas about the kinds of pictures they want and so will be prepared to wait to view the completed film to see if it meets their specified criteria – and these criteria will vary from year to year, according to changes in the market.

FESTIVALS

The principle aims of screening a film at a festival are to reach potential buyers who, for whatever reason, did not buy the film at an earlier stage – and also to reach the press and sometimes even the public.

As discussed in Section Three, selling non-English-language films prior to completion is usually very difficult for most territories. The festival screening will represent the first, and perhaps only, opportunity to interest buyers in such films and for this reason is of vital importance and will require the same kind of careful preparation that goes into a market screening.

Jan

Palm Springs International Film Festival (California, USA)
11 days early Jan
Tel: 1-619/328.34.56.

Sundance Film Festival (Park City, USA)
11 days
Tel:1-801/328.34.56.

Brussels International Film Festival (Belgium)
10 days mid Jan
Tel: 32-2/218.10.55.

Rotterdam Film Festival (Netherlands)
12 days end Jan
Tel: 31-10/411.80.80.

Awards:
Golden Globes (Hollywood Foreign Press Association Awards)

Feb

Göteborg Film Festival (Sweden)
10 days early Feb
Tel: 46-31/41.05.46.

Monte-Carlo International TV Festival and Market (Monaco)
7 days early Feb
Tel: 33/93.30.49.44.

Berlin International Film Festival (Germany)
12 days mid Feb
Tel: 49-30/254.892.25.

AFM **American Film Market** (Los Angeles, USA)
10 days end Feb
Tel: 1-310/447.15.55.

Nominations:
BAFTA (UK)
CESARS (France)
GOYAS (Spain)
OSCARS (USA)

May

CANNES **Cannes International Film Festival and Market** (France)
12 days mid May

Tel: - Official selection : 33-1/42.66.92.20.
      - Director's Fortnight: 33-1/45.61.01.66.
      - International Film Market: 33-1/44.13.40.40.

Jun

Midnight Sun Film Festival (Sodankylä, Finland)
5 days
Tel: 358-96/.93.21.008.

Troia International Film Festival (Portugal)
10 days early June
Tel: 351-65/441.21.

Cinema Expo International (Brussels, Belgium)
4 days end June
Tel: 32-2/478.31.97.

Munich Film Festival (Germany)
7 days end June
Tel: 49-89/381.90.40.

Mysfest Film Festival (Cattolica, Italy)
8 days end June
Tel: 39-54/967.802.

Awards:
DAVID DI DONATELLO (Italy)

Sep

Deauville US Film Festival (France) 10 days early Sept
Tel: 33-1/46.40.55.00.

Telluride Film Festival (USA) 4 days early Sept
Tel: 1-603/643.12.55.

Toronto Festival of Festivals (Canada) 10 days
Tel: 1-416/967.73.71.

Venice International Film Festival (Italy) 12 days early Sept
Tel: 39-41/52.18.711.

San Sebastian International Film Festival (Spain)
10 days mid Sept. Tel: 34-43/481.212.

Dutch Film Days (Utrecht, Netherlands) 10 days end Sept
Tel: 31-30/32.26.84.

IFFM International Feature Film Market (USA) 9 days end Sept
Tel: 1-212/243.77.77.

Tokyo International Film Festival and Market (Japan)
11 days end Sept
Tel: 81-3/35.63.63.05.

Oct

New York Film Festival (USA) 17 days early Oct
Tel: 1-212/875.56.10.

Vancouver International Film Festival (Canada)
17 days early Oct
Tel: 1-604/685.02.60.

Ghent International Film Festival of Flanders (Belgium)
12 days mid Oct
Tel: 32-9/221.89.46.

MIPCOM International TV and video market (Cannes, France)
5 days mid Oct
Tel: 33-1/44.34.44.44.

MIFED **MIFED** International Film Market (Milan, Italy) 6 days end Oct
Tel: 39-2/48.01.29.12.

Valladollid International Film Festival (Spain)
9 days end Oct
Tel: 34-83/305.700

 **Mar**

NATO/Showest Convention for US distributors, exhibitors
(Las Vegas, USA)
4 days early March
Tel: 1-310/657.77.24

Awards:
BAFTA
CESARS
GOYAS
OSCARS

 **Apr**

Istanbul International Film Festival (Turkey)
16 days early April
Tel: 90-1/260.45.33.

MIP-TV International TV & Video Market (Cannes, France)
6 days mid April
Tel: 33-1/44.34.44.44

 **Jul**

Karlovy Vary International Film Festival (Czech Republic)
Tel: 42-27.58.14.23.

Moscow International Film Festival (Russia)
Biannual event
12 days early July
Tel: 7-095/297.76.45.

Taormina Film Festival (Italy)
7 days end July
Tel: 39-6/322.64.13.

Aug

Locarno International Film Festival (Switzerland)
11 days early August
Tel: 41-93/310.232.

Edinburgh International Film Festival (UK)
16 days mid August
Tel: 44-31/228.40.51.

Haugesund Film Festival (Norway)
7 days end August
Tel: 47-4/734.300.

Montreal World Film Festival (Canada)
12 days end August
Tel: 1-514/933.96.99.

 **Nov**

London Film Festival (UK)
18 days early Nov
Tel: 44-71/815.13.25

Sarasota French Film Festival (Florida, USA)
6 days mid Nov
Tel: 1-813/351.90.10

 **Dec**

Cairo International Film Festival (Egypt)
10 days early Dec
Tel: 202/393.89.79.

Havana International Film Festival (Cuba)
late Dec
Tel: 53-7/34.400.

Awards:
Felix (Best European films of the year)

CALENDAR OF MAJOR EVENTS IN THE FILM YEAR

The marketing materials which will accompany a festival screening are, in essence, the same as those used for screening the film at a market, although the target audience will be somewhat wider, since in many cases the public will also be attending.

A festival screening will, in many cases, mark the first time that the critics have had a chance to review the picture. The reviews from those critics will be particularly important in determining the likely success of arthouse films at the box office. A poor review from an influential critic for such a film in a particular country will invariably hurt the box office, while a good review can substantially enhance the saleability of films which otherwise appear to have very few tangible marketing hooks.[4]

The fact that members of the public are able to attend most of the annual film festivals around the world means that the festival screening will often be the first time that the picture is seen by the general audience. The reaction of the public will also have an impact on the subsequent performance of the film. If the audience likes the film, it will be likely to recommend the film to friends and colleagues, generating favourable word of mouth prior to the film's release, and boosting its chances of success. Conversely, a poor reception by a festival audience will invariably hinder the film's subsequent performance at the box office since word of mouth will be poor.[5]

CANNES INTERNATIONAL FILM FESTIVAL

The most important film festival is the Festival International du Film, also known as the Cannes International Film Festival, held together with the film market, over a 12-day period each May. Screenings at Cannes are restricted to those with special passes or invitations and, as with most film festivals, are divided into a number of different sections. Before entering a film for consideration for a festival screening at Cannes, the sales agent or distributor will need to have a high level of confidence in the production, since a bad reception at Cannes can paralyse a film's chances of success. In many cases the film will be reviewed by many of the most influential critics from high-profile consumer and trade publications around the world, so bad reviews can fast become universal. The film must also be strong enough to stand out from the competition as many hundreds of films will be screened during the festival and market.

4 For more on the role of the critic see Section Five: Film Distribution in Europe.

5 For further analysis of the importance of word of mouth see Section Five: Film Distribution in Europe.

The distributor or sales agent must also decide which section of Cannes will be most appropriate for a given title. The most prestigious section of the festival is the Official Selection, which includes films being shown *in competition* for the prize of the Palme D'Or, a handful of titles shown *out of competition*, and some 25 smaller, more intimate films in the section Un Certain Regard. The films chosen for the Official competition will have the highest profile during the festival, since they will each receive a gala screening which will invariably be attended by leading figures from all sections of the film industry (ranging from actors and actresses to potential distributors) as well as by journalists from the print media and television. The Official competition will usually consist of a mix of titles, ranging from mainstream commercial pictures to more specialised arthouse films.

The other important section at Cannes is la Quinzaine des Réalisateurs (Director's Fortnight), which tends to screen smaller, more intimate films than those in the Official Selection. Entering a film in this section may ensure that a title has a better chance to shine, rather than competing with the high-profile titles which will dominate the Official competition.

Entering Cannes is like a competition in itself, as over 600 films are seen by festival director Gilles Jacob and his team before they decide on the 25 or 30 films that will be screened at the festival. All the selections at Cannes are made by the official organising committee, which is based in Paris, and headed by Jacob. Establishing a good professional relationship with Jacob and his colleague Pierre Viot is of vital importance in helping a film's chances of being entered for competition at Cannes. Jacob in particular is in regular contact with sales agents and distributors from around the world during the course of the 12 months leading up to each Cannes festival, looking for potential festival contenders. In most cases, the decision as to which films are selected for Cannes is not made until approximately one month before the festival opens, so the distributor has to move very quickly to put together marketing materials, such as filmographies and brochures.

If a film receives a favourable response at a Cannes festival screening, favourable reports will travel very rapidly around the festival by word of mouth. Potential buyers of the film will soon be heading to the office of the film's distributor so that, as with the market screening, they will need to ensure that all marketing materials have been carefully prepared in advance.

Going to Cannes in competition is also a costly business. As a guide, the costs are likely to be at least $75,000 (ECU67,000) and if budgets permit, could be far more.

KEY POINTS

THE FIRST MARKET

- Shooting script. Should be neatly bound and presented.

- A short (three paragraphs) and a long (one to two pages) synopsis of the film.

- Biographies and filmographies of major cast and crew. Box-office figures for the previous films featuring the director and major cast.

- Press release. Gives outline details of the film including director, cast, principal crew, film's budget and the start of principal photography, who is handling international sales and the genre of the film.

- Press conference. Gives the media the opportunity to interview the director and stars.

- Announcing ad. Published in one of the trade papers, and gives details of the forthcoming production.

THE SECOND MARKET

- A production schedule and the date of delivery to the US distributor, if any.

- Office displays including posters. A vital tool in establishing the visual image of the film. Should emphasise key elements of film.

- Stills. Best stills are those secured while film is shooting. May be difficult and certainly costly to obtain photographs later.

- A showreel on film or video containing footage from film. Somewhere between 5 and 15 minutes in length.

- A rough cut of the trailer. Anywhere from 30 seconds to three minutes in length.

- Brochures. Expensive, but valuable marketing tool especially at festivals.

THE THIRD MARKET

- Trade advertising. Used to promote completed film to distributors.

- Organisation of market screening(s) for a film. The climax of the sales campaign. Should be heavily promoted in the trade press and held during the middle of the market.

- Press book. Aimed at both the consumer and the trade press and designed to maximise interest in the film.

OTHER FESTIVALS

The other key festivals include the Berlin, held in February, Venice, which is held in September, and Tokyo, later the same month. Like Cannes, these festivals will generally only consider films which have not yet screened at other festivals and which have been released in few, if any, territories. There are many hundreds of other film festivals, of varying importance, held around the world.[6] In some cases, a sales agent may choose to enter a film in a lesser-known festival where it will have a greater chance of standing out, rather than in an event where it might be swamped by a deluge of high-profile films.

In many cases, the sales agent for a film will work in close conjunction with the local distributor for a film when trying to get a film selected for a particular festival. For the local distributor, the festival screening will offer an important opportunity to raise the profile of the title in their own territory.

In the case of the most prestigious festivals, the sales agent will usually attend the event. For others, where the film has primarily been entered to boost awareness in the particular territory where the festival is being held, the sales agent will not attend, since it will often be the local distributor who will have decided to enter the film in a particular event.

This section has examined the importance of markets and festivals as a means of selling the film to distributors, of securing press coverage and of making initial contact with the target audience. Once the film has been sold, the distributor will start to implement a marketing strategy, which may involve building on some of these elements, but which will be much wider in scope. In the following section, we will examine the tools which the distributor uses to maximise the effectiveness of the marketing strategy in the run-up to the film's release.

6 See Calendar of Markets and Festivals p.72/73.

FILM DISTRIBUTION IN EUROPE

**" Awareness of a film does
not simply materialise from
thin air but has to be created
in a process which involves
utilising marketing tools. "**

This section deals with distribution in Europe and the ways in which distributors motivate the general public to pay to see a film on the big screen. For each individual film, the distributor must arrive at the marketing strategy with the best possible chance of maximising the audience for the film.

As emphasised in Section One, distributors must have a means of attracting the consumer to their particular films in the face of competition from other films, from other leisure activities and even from other forms of audiovisual entertainment such as video and television which, in many cases, will be cheaper and more convenient for the consumer. Film distribution is a business seeking to maximise its share of a limited pot of consumer expenditure and leisure time.

Going to the movies is a leisure activity. Therefore, the level of demand for individual films will be influenced by competition for the consumers' leisure time from activities such as theatre going, sports and television.

This section will address the strategies used by the distributor to attract the audience into the cinema. But before doing so, it is necessary to examine the environment in which distributors in various European countries operate.

KEY CONCEPTS IN FILM DISTRIBUTION

ATTRACTING THE PUBLIC

Since every film involves a unique combination of elements, the marketing of individual pictures, unlike the marketing of many other goods, cannot rely simply on consumer preference for certain tried and tested ingredients. Although there may be some desire on the part of the audience to see a film because of star names, content or occasionally the director.

In the case of sequels to successful films, there will be an opportunity to build on the audience's taste for an earlier film. However, the value of such "brand names" in selling a film is never assured, as there are so many other elements (personal recommendation, reviews and so on) which will determine audience demand for a specific picture.

There are certain films or film makers which have managed to create a brand name value, but they are relatively few in number. In many cases, Walt Disney, the Hollywood studio, is able to use the perceived value of the Disney brand name to help sell its films, since the studio has a reputation for producing high-quality, entertaining films for children, particularly animated features.

The films from the pairing of producer Ismail Merchant and director James Ivory are another example of identifiable branding, based around the fact that they specialise in period literary adaptations featuring quality production values. The term "Merchant/ Ivory production" connotes a specific type of film (A Room With A View, A Passage to India, Howard's End), which is likely to have a clearly defined target audience. Films from the Spanish director Pedro Almodovar also have a particular cinematic style, that has in effect become the equivalent of a brand name.

> **"A cinema audience does not usually buy cinema tickets based on the appeal of national brands, with perhaps the exception of the Hollywood movie."**

Unlike purveyors of other goods, the film distributor cannot usually rely on the country of origin of the film as a selling point. Although people may decide to go out for an Italian meal or prefer Belgian beer, a cinema audience does not usually buy cinema tickets based on the appeal of national brands – with perhaps the exception of the Hollywood movie. As a rule, in film, unlike many other businesses, the name of the supplier (in this case the distributor) is virtually irrelevant to the marketing process, where the whole focus is on the individual film.

CONVERTING AWARENESS INTO WANT TO SEE

The primary task for the distributor is to define the target audience for a film, and then to create and sustain the *awareness* of the film by that target audience, so that it knows that the film is being released, and has some idea of its most appealing elements. This awareness then has to be translated into *want to see*, so that rather than just knowing about the film, the audience has a desire to pay to view it on the big screen.

BUILDING WORD OF MOUTH

Awareness of a film does not simply materialise from thin air but has to be created, in a process which involves utilising advertising, *word of mouth* (meaning that the desire to see a film is stimulated by personal recommendation), reviews and many other strategies. It is more difficult to create want to see, because the desire to actually see a film will be heavily dependent on subjective judgements made by the cinema-going public.

Word of mouth, the opinion of a person on a film and its potential influence on other potential cinema goers who haven't seen the film is a very (if not the most) powerful instrument in a film's theatrical life. Even if a film opens well, poor or negative word of mouth is likely to kill any long-term box-office success.

The key for the distributor seeking to build word of mouth is to determine, before a film's release, the kind of people who will be most influential in spreading good or bad opinions. These opinion formers can be people working within the industry (distributors, exhibitors, designers etc) who represent the first audience, as well as the media, which has an influence over the general public, or specific consumer target groups (see section on Market Research, p.142).

Once the film has opened, the distributor can tell very quickly from the box-office results if it has been successfully positioned so as to reach the avid cinema goers and to convert awareness into want to see. During the second week of release, the percentage drop in admissions will be a crucial indicator of the film's likely playing time; the steeper the drop, the shorter the period for which the exhibitor is likely to want to play the film.

Few films have the luxury of being able to grow popular with time – arthouse films, in particular, since exhibitors or bookers will rarely have the confidence to let such films grow over time. It is therefore essential that as many opinion formers as possible should be attracted to the cinema, ideally in the opening week (or weekend), so that they can recommend the film to their peers.

The distributor will set out to maximise awareness, want to see and word of mouth through the creation of a marketing plan designed to enable a film to reach its audience, a process known as the *positioning* of a film.[1]

POSITIONING

Just as one of the tasks of the sales agent is to position the film to the international buyers in the industry, so the distributor must find the best way of positioning the film for its potential audience. The nature of a particular film will be an important factor in this. The process of positioning a mainstream thriller, likely to appeal

---

1 The American research group Marketcast uses the term "avids" to define those cinema goers who will play a crucial role in determining word of mouth (see p.142ff for further details).

" There are very few European stars with names big enough to act as the central marketing hook for a picture, even though their names may have some value in the country in which the film originated. "

to a broad audience, is very different from the approach used for an intimate drama from an arthouse director. While in most cases the marketing budget available for the mainstream picture will be very much higher than for the arthouse film, this is by no means the sole distinction between selling the two titles to the cinema goer. The style of the poster, the marketing hooks used to entice the audience and the advertising media are all likely to be different.

The effort and skill required to position a small film effectively can be considerably greater than that required for a much larger film, since the former involves targeting specialised audiences, which may be difficult to achieve through conventional channels. It may also be harder to identify those elements of a film which are likely to appeal to such audiences.

The task of the distributor positioning such films is also made harder by the fact that, in most cases, such films will not feature stars known to an international audience. There are very few European stars with names big enough to act as the central marketing hook for a picture, even though their names may have some value in the country in which the film originated.

Having defined the key concepts that shape the approach of the distributor, it is time to look at some of the strategies used by distributors as a means of attempting to create the largest possible audience for a specific title. However, before doing that, it will be necessary to define the general context of film distribution in Europe.

THE STRUCTURE OF FILM DISTRIBUTION IN EUROPE

In 1991 the distribution arms of the US majors accounted, on average, for 72.5% of box-office revenues in each local market. Each studio tends to release between 20 and 35 pictures a year, most of which are produced by their own production arm, but some of the films will be *negative pick-ups*, where the film has been acquired from independent producers, once it has completed principal photography or at some stage during post-production.

While some US studios, such as Columbia Tri-Star, 20th Century Fox and Warner Brothers, usually use their own distribution arms to handle their pictures internationally, others have formed joint ventures to distribute their films overseas. Outside the US, most films from Paramount, Universal and MGM are released through United International Pictures (UIP), while the overseas distribution arm of Disney, in most European territories, is Buena Vista International. In France, Disney has set up a joint-venture partnership with Gaumont, an independent distributor.

The bulk of the other films released in Europe are handled by a few large local distribution companies that release between 10 and 30 titles a year. The major national independents like AMLF in France, Penta in Italy, Guild in the UK, Lauren Films in Spain and Independent in Belgium, usually have formal **output deals** (or a rather looser informal alliance) with at least one indigenous production company and with several international sales companies. An output deal means that a distribution company strikes an agreement with an international sales company or with a producer, giving the distributor rights to a number of pictures over a period of time.

This makes the task of the sales company or producer easier since they no longer have to be concerned about finding a distributor for the specified pictures in specific territories. From the distributors' viewpoint, it gives guaranteed access to a slate of films against which they can amortise their overheads. Distributors who do not have the benefit of an output deal with specific companies constantly have to ensure that they are acquiring enough pictures to distribute and make a return on their investment.

Film distribution is a high-risk business, since just a handful of titles will enjoy substantial profits, while most pictures lose money on their theatrical run. The task facing distributors is to try to ensure that they have a sufficiently broad spread of films so that the profits from a handful of successful pictures will outweigh any losses incurred by other films.

Other than the US majors and the large local distributors, the remainder of the market is controlled by distributors specialising in arthouse films or re-releases. In France and Germany there tends to be a larger number of small, niche distributors handling perhaps just two or three films a year. In the UK, a considerable number of independent distributors have hit financial difficulty and only a few substantial independents, including Guild and Rank Film Distributors, remain to challenge the US studios.

For the independent distributor it is important to have a sound understanding of the competitive advantages enjoyed by the US majors, as this will help in designing marketing and distribution strategies which offer an effective alternative to the Hollywood studios.

STRENGTHS OF THE US MAJORS

So what are some of the structural factors that enable the US distributors to maintain their market position, and what impact do they have on the independent distributor? Five major strengths can be identified.

ECONOMIES OF SCALE

As explained in Section Three, the Hollywood studios have a vertically-integrated structure, spanning development, production, distribution and, in some cases, exhibition, which guarantees them access to a constant flow of major pictures. This volume of films enables them to spread their risk across a large number of films, so that the rewards from a few highly profitable pictures easily outweigh the losses from other films.

The fact that the US studios are able to guarantee a certain volume of high-profile pictures each year will also give them greater leverage in negotiating terms with the cinema chains, on issues such as dates of release, known as *playdates*. The ability to exercise control over when a film is released can be crucial, since certain weeks of the year, such as particular holiday periods, may be especially favourable for releasing a film while other time slots will be much weaker. It depends on the type of picture and in which country it is being released.

> " The ability to exercise control over when a film is released can be crucial. "

Since the rate-card price of the prints and advertising (P&A) tools to communicate with the audience are the same for independents and the US majors, and the US majors will often be buying in bulk for a guaranteed supply of films, this gives them considerable negotiating strength with suppliers in this sphere. The rapidly rising costs of release, of prints and advertising materials, have also hit the independents hard.

By contrast, most independent distributors in Europe, even allowing for any output deals they might have, cannot guarantee the exhibitors a steady stream of films over a long period of time; they are usually dependent on acquiring their films from independent third parties and are often unable to rely on receiving the films at a given time. Independents in Europe have much less leverage than the majors when it comes to exerting pressure on producers to meet a target release date.

PAN-EUROPEAN MARKETING OPERATIONS

The US majors also benefit from horizontal integration. They operate large distribution structures on an international scale with offices in virtually every territory they serve around the world. This enables them to co-ordinate their marketing across a large number of countries and make economies of scale in areas such as market researches and *star junkets*.

Although there are almost as many screens in Europe as there are in the US, in Europe they are scattered across 30 different countries. This means creating different campaigns for different audiences with different languages. Because of their co-ordinated network offices, the US studios are able to centralise the release of the film across several territories.

For the independent distributor any delay in obtaining prints and marketing tools from either the producer or the sales agent can significantly hurt the performance of the film.

To maximise the chances of success at the box office, the producer and sales agent must deliver materials to the distributor on time. Independent European distributors usually have one or two people responsible for chasing the marketing tools (photos, posters, brochures, advertising campaign material etc) and most have expressed dissatisfaction over the fact that such material nearly always arrives late. Good *servicing* is thus another key element in the positioning of a film in its various markets and should not be neglected.

CONCENTRATION ON A FEW STAR-DRIVEN TITLES

The bulk of the box-office revenues in each European territory is concentrated on 20 or so films that attract some 50% of the total admissions.[2] Most of these pictures are star-driven films distributed by the US studios.

The dominance of the US majors is based not on the volume of pictures they release, since in many cases the combined number of pictures released by local distributors is considerably greater than that handled by the studios. For instance, in 1991, in the UK, the majors accounted for only 39% of the total number of films released, yet these titles accounted for 66% of total box-office rev-

2 Source: CNC, France.

enues.[3] This demonstrates that the strength of the distribution operations of the US majors is based on the high level of success achieved by a relatively small number of titles, while the smaller revenues achieved by independents are generated by a larger number of films.

The US majors may release between 20-35 pictures in a given year. Just a few, sufficiently large winners at the box office, like Basic Instinct or Jurassic Park, for example (of which the latter made more money in four weeks than the 16 other UIP pictures released in the first eight months of 1993), will result in handsome profits. Film distribution is like roulette – there's no guarantee of success and the profits from one win can easily outstrip the costs of a string of losses. The independents, with some notable exceptions, do not have access to the high-earning, star-driven films, although they may well have pictures which are capable of more limited commercial success in the marketplace.[4]

> " **Film distribution is like roulette, there's no guarantee of success and the profits from one win can easily outstrip the costs of a string of losses.** "

In many cases, the independents will be using the marketing exposure they gain from theatrical release as a loss-leader for the film, offsetting these losses against the money they will make from the video and television release of the film.

But the fall-off in the levels of growth of the video market has affected the independents. When video rental was stronger, many European independents were able to survive on so-called B-movies which did not feature well-known stars or a name director, yet had a clearly identifiable genre, usually action-adventure. But at the end of the 1980s, the video rental market began to change, so that the kind of titles that succeeded on video were much closer to those that did well in the cinema – high-quality films featuring known stars and directors. As a result, in many instances, independents were no longer able to rely on video as a means of offsetting losses incurred on theatrical distribution. Although the emergence of new media, such as pay-TV,[5] has pro-

---

3 Figures cited in the British Film Institute Yearbook 1993, based on information supplied by Entertainment Data Inc.

4 Exceptions to this would include the blockbuster films produced by Carolco, which are released, for example, by the independent distributor Guild in the UK.

5 In the last few years pay-TV, encouraged by the phenomenal success of Canal + in France, has flourished throughout Europe. Major pay-TV operations in Europe include British Sky Broadcasting (BSkyB) in the UK, Premiere in Germany (part-owned by Canal +) and Canal + España (also part owned by the French-based service).

vided some compensation for the decline in video rental, the films which succeed with pay-TV audiences also tend to be the star-driven films.

But it should not be assumed that simply because the US studios have these strategic advantages, the position of the European distributor is hopeless. Rather, for all the reasons cited above – and not just the greater financial resources available to the US majors – the strategies deployed by independent distributors for maximising the effectiveness of their films will be very different from those used by the studios.

The US majors will frequently use costly advertising campaigns across a variety of media (newspapers, magazines, television, radio, advertising hoardings and any other available means) to ensure that international audiences are aware of their films.

The cost of such campaigns means that they remain well beyond the financial means of most European distributors. But for the latter, the efficient and creative use of resources are critical weapons which can be used to compensate for limited budgets. The sheer volume of money thrown at a marketing campaign is, after all, not necessarily an index of its effectiveness. The use of subtlety and humour, combined with a close understanding of local audiences by European distributors can often be considerably more cost-effective than an expensive hard-sell approach.

STRATEGIES FOR MARKETING AND DISTRIBUTING FILMS TO THE AUDIENCE

As we have stressed throughout this book, every film is unique and requires specific marketing strategies to create awareness and want to see, and the methods which are used to achieve this can be clearly identified. To determine a particular approach for a specific film, a distributor planning a release campaign will set out to answer a number of questions which will usually include the following:

• How should the film be positioned?

- What are the elements of the film that have strong marketing potential?

- What is the target audience for the picture and does it have the ability to cross over to other audiences?

- What is the optimum time for releasing the film?

- How much should be spent on prints and advertising?

- How is the film best promoted in terms of paid advertising, publicity and promotion?

The following sections address each of these questions in turn.

POSITIONING THE FILM

It is the task of the film distributor in each territory, often working in conjunction with the film's producer (and in some territories, the director), to position the film in a way which will maximise the level of awareness and want to see among the target audience. How do they set about doing this?

Distributors must first determine the type of film that they are selling to the public, since this will be a critical element in the positioning of the picture, helping to determine the target audience and influencing the entire style of the marketing campaign. For example, the poster campaign, the trailer and the promotional tie-ins used for a mainstream horror film will emphasise very different elements from those used for an intimate arthouse drama. Some films may combine elements of several genres, for instance a thriller with a strong love interest, allowing the distributor to simultaneously position the film for two distinct types of audience.

In other cases, the name of the director may signify that the film is clearly an arthouse film – one that will appeal to a specialised audience, which will be primarily composed of relatively affluent, educated people living in urban areas.

In many cases, it will be relatively easy to determine the nature of a film, based on the ingredients of the story which may refer to the conventions of a specific genre. In the case of films handled by the US majors, once the film has been identified as belonging to a specific category (e.g. romantic comedy) it will usually be possible to determine the way in which the film will be positioned for audiences throughout Europe.

If, however, the audience finds it difficult to identify the genre of the film, it may indicate that the distributor is uncertain as to what type of picture it is that is being sold. Unconvincing positioning of a film will have a negative effect on the consumer's perception of the film, and may hurt box-office performance.

Defining the genre – even multiple genres – is the first step on the way to positioning the film.

The specific nature of the marketing campaign may differ from country to country, but the generic positioning in different countries will be broadly similar since the elements of a particular film will tend to appeal to the same target group in most European territories. Since the release of a given film across the various European territories is usually staggered, this similarity in the way the film is positioned enables the distribution arms of the Hollywood studios to learn from the reaction to the film in one territory, when preparing the film for release elsewhere.

> " Unconvincing positioning of a film will have a negative effect on the consumer's perception of the film, and may hurt box-office performance. "

By contrast, it may be harder for independent distributors to determine how to position a film for a particular country, since some of the pictures they handle may be perceived as mainstream pictures in one territory and yet will be treated as an arthouse picture in another. This is because the elements of the film, such as the stars or the subject matter, for example, often do not have the same universal appeal as the corresponding ingredients in a Hollywood film. A mainstream European film may have a considerable appeal on home territory, but is likely to attract only small audiences elsewhere.

For example, Cyrano de Bergerac, starring Gérard Depardieu, was perceived as a mainstream film in France, because the subject matter and the cast were likely to appeal to a broad audience. Yet the appeal of those same elements outside France was more limited. As a result, in other countries the film was effectively treated as an arthouse release, or in some cases, as with the UK and Spain, it became a *cross-over picture* and attracted a significant mainstream audience.

> " The independent distributor must take particular care to ensure that the appropriate target audience for a film has been identified. "

The independent distributor must take particular care to ensure that the appropriate target audience for a film has been identified. The distributor should not simply assume that the way in which a film was positioned in one country will be appropriate for another territory, since the elements of the film may carry a very different appeal in other countries.

POSITIONING PICTURES WHICH DON'T FIT TRADITIONAL CATEGORIES

Distributors of all kinds, especially independent distributors, will often find themselves handling films which do not fit neatly into the categories of either arthouse or commercial film. For instance, there are arthouse pictures which have the potential to be cross-over pictures, meaning that they may also be able to reach more commercial audiences. Recent examples of such pictures might include Delicatessen, Howard's End and Jamón Jamón.

Equally, there are commercial films, usually falling into the $5-$15 million budget range, and featuring known stars and a director, which once completed may turn out to be insufficiently commercial for a wide release and yet not specialised enough for releasing in arthouse cinemas. The distributor will often have bought these films at the script stage or while the film was in *pre-production*, anticipating that it would be suitable for a wide theatrical release.

On paper the film's ingredients, such as the story, the stars and the track record of the director, may have indicated that the film had commercial potential. But on viewing the completed film the distributor may realise that the money spent on wide theatrical release is unlikely to be recouped at the cinema. However, in order to maximise the video potential of the film a small theatrical release will create vital exposure which may eventually enable the picture to recoup its costs. In some cases, there will be a contractual obligation for a distributor to release a film theatrically, prior to its appearance on video, simply in order to secure this exposure.

In such cases, the distributor will need to create a cost-effective campaign built on certain core elements, such as the appeal of the stars for example, while also ensuring that other elements of the film, such as a particularly unusual storyline, are used to try to broaden the audience for the film. The aim is not only to reach the general public but also to influence the video distributors and to help promote the title when it is eventually shipped out to video rental shops.

MARKETING POTENTIAL: FIVE KEY ELEMENTS

When selling a film to the public, there are many elements which can be used to make it attractive to the public. It is the task of the distributor to identify these elements and translate them into an effective marketing campaign. The ability to find and then exploit these elements is a skill which can often go a long way towards overcoming the constraints caused by a limited marketing budget.

Five key elements have been singled out below which can be used to help sell a picture.

EXPLOITING THE VALUE OF A FILM'S ASSETS

The stars and/or the director of a film are a crucial selling point for many mainstream commercial films, as well as for some arthouse films. Their names will frequently help secure publicity for the film, which may be particularly useful in the case of films which do not have a large prints and advertising budget, as such films will be more dependent on reviews and press coverage.

However it will always be easier to secure coverage if the stars or director are well known, since their names will help publishers to achieve their goal of maximising magazine or newspaper sales, or help a television programme to boost its ratings.

STARS

The mere presence of a star is no guarantee of box-office success, but a star name will often be the central plank of a publicity and advertising campaign since this will give the distributor the best chance of maximising awareness of the film among the target audience. If the stars of a film are judged to be of value in selling a film they will feature heavily in the poster campaign, in the trailer for the film, as well as in any radio or television advertising. The distributor will also try to persuade the star to tour individual territories to promote the film and to give interviews to the media so that the film secures widespread editorial coverage.[6]

> "The mere presence of a star is no guarantee of box-office success."

If a star will not tour, an alternative is to arrange telephone interviews or to fly a star to a prominent festival and arrange interviews there with local and foreign press.

The popular press and best-selling magazines will frequently be targeted when trying to secure interviews with stars, as most films with well-known stars will be aimed at readers of these types of publications.

While American stars, such as Kevin Costner or Sharon Stone, have massive box-office appeal, on a more limited scale there are some European stars who have the ability to attract audiences,

---

6 The ways in which such goals can be achieved is dealt with in the section headed The Essential Ingredients of an Advertising Campaign (p.127ff).

such as Juliette Binoche, Gérard Depardieu and Anthony Hopkins. However, other than a small handful of names, the value of European stars will usually be confined to their home territories.[7] For example, the Italian star Roberto Benigni was a major factor in the success of Johnny Stecchino in Italy, but the film failed to attract a significant audience in the few European territories where it was released.[8]

Over half the people surveyed in a recent poll of Italian cinema goers said that a film's cast affects their decision as to whether or not they will go and see a film; just over one-third attached some importance to the name of the director.[9] The specific appeal of an actor or an actress in a particular film is determined by a number of factors, including their previous work, and also any other films in which they appear which are released at approximately the same time.[10] The success of films such as Delicatessen or My Life as a Dog, which do not feature big names, has demonstrated that it is possible for pictures to achieve popularity with audiences, despite the absence of well-known names.

The stars are important in helping the theatrical performance of a film, but they can help also boost the awareness and eventual performance when the film is released in the ancillary markets.

THE DIRECTOR

In Europe, the name of the director can be particularly important in helping to create audience appeal. In most cases, the director's name is most important when marketing an arthouse film to relatively well-educated, urban audiences. The name of the director will usually have particular appeal in the country of origin, but there will also be more limited appeal in other territories.

The director's name may feature prominently in the poster campaign and in the trailer for the film. As with well-known stars, the distributor may try to persuade the director to tour individual territories to promote the film and to give interviews to the media,

7 Most of those European names that do have box-office value across a number of European countries usually have received an enormous boost from the fact that they have received exposure in successful Hollywood films. The name of Gérard Depardieu was boosted by the success of Green Card, while the profile of Anthony Hopkins benefited enormously from the success of The Silence of the Lambs.

8 It has been argued in some quarters that the absence of European stars has been a major factor in the decline in the box-office share of European pictures, since it deprives films of a major marketing hook.

9 Source: Identikit dello Spettatore Cinematografico Italiano, published by ANICA. the Italian film trade organisation.

10 In such cases, the star can benefit from considerable media exposure. For example, Romane Bohringer was suddenly put in the spotlight in France because of her part in Les Nuits Fauves and L'Accompagnatrice.

although the target media for such coverage may be quite different from that used for star interviews. It will usually be the arts sections of the serious newspapers or the heavyweight magazines which will be interested in interviewing the director.

The names of a few European directors such as Carlos Saura and Wim Wenders will act as a hook for audiences throughout Europe, but such directors are the exception to the rule. In either case, using the director's name gives a certain brand value to the film in the eyes of its potential audience. It acts as a pointer to the audience that, based on their knowledge of previous work by that director, they are about to watch a certain kind of film.

But even if the names of the stars and directors are not enough in themselves to create a high level of want to see, they can often be extremely useful in raising awareness of the title among the targetted *primary audience*.

EXPLOITING THE GENRE AND STORY INGREDIENTS

Regardless of the identity of the director and the stars of the film itself, it is the combination of the performances, the script and the production values which will usually be the largest factor in determining the eventual success or failure of a film.

The distributor aims to use the genre of the film (e.g. action thriller, romantic comedy, period drama) as a market hook so that the audience knows what kind of film it can expect. The aim is not to give the story away but to tell the audience that they can expect, say, a comedy rather than a psychological drama.

The design of the poster campaign and the trailer will clearly reflect the genre of the film if this is felt to be a particularly strong selling point. By using particular images from the film, the distributor will be able to signal to the target audience that the picture belongs to a genre with which they are familiar and which they may be expected to enjoy. It is not only the visual image on the poster but also the quotes used from reviewers which can help reinforce the impression that a film belongs to a particular genre. Most Hollywood films operate within specific genre categories which can be identified with relative ease. In many cases, it is much harder to classify European films within such precise generic boundaries. Many films produced in Europe are more personal in style, a reflection of the fact that the director often has a much greater level of influence on the treatment of the subject matter than is usually the case in the US. This can make it harder to position some films in terms of genre.

> " **It is harder to classify European films in terms of genre.** "

In these cases the name of the director may be a more effective way of making the audience aware of the kind of film they can expect, since as discussed in the preceding section, the audience will have certain expectations about the style of film based on the identity of the director.

There is one particular type of film that can easily be identified in generic terms, and that is comedy. These films perform very strongly at the box office within their country of origin but achieve limited impact abroad. Examples of such films would include Johnny Stecchino, which grossed $24m (ECU21.5m) in its native Italy; Les Visiteurs, which grossed $67m (ECU59.63m) in France (figures up to 6/10/93), and Den Ofrivillige Golfaren (The Accidental Golfer), which in its home country of Sweden grossed $10.4m (ECU9.35m). Often such films will perform much more strongly in their native territories than many US films.

Another clearly identifiable European genre is the literary adaptation, which often has cross-over potential with foreign audiences. Such films include Cyrano de Bergerac, based on the original Rostand play, House of Spirits, based on Isabel Allende's novel, and the adaptations by Merchant/Ivory of the novels of E.M. Forster, including A Room With a View and Howard's End. The publicity and promotional materials for such films will usually draw prominent attention to the fact that the film is based on literary source material. This will help attract those who are already familiar with the original work. It also helps to implant a certain impression of quality in the mind of the audience, since it is usually assumed that literary adaptations will employ high-quality production values and conform to a certain level of taste.

Sequels to a successful film, which exploit a successful, tested formula, are also a well-established and often highly profitable segment of the film industry. Such films are frequently based around a particular character, and examples of those which have spawned one or more sequels in Europe would include such pictures as Don Camillo in France, the Sissi films in Germany and the Toto series in Italy. In Hollywood, sequels are, if anything, even more important to the workings of the industry, as is demonstrated by, for example, the Nightmare on Elm Street and Police Academy series.

For the distributor, the mere fact of a film being a sequel to a successful original is a strong selling point. The marketing campaign for the film will be able to exploit the similarity between the two pictures, persuading the audience that they will have a chance once more to enjoy many of the elements which drew them to the original film, but in the context of a fresh story.

When marketing a sequel, the distributor will also have a much clearer idea of the core audience for the film, based on the audience for the original film. This will make it easier to position the film, in terms of creating a marketing concept and also in terms of selecting the advertising media which will be most effective in reaching the target audience.

In some cases, however, the distributor will also be looking to attract those people who did not see the original film, and so will be looking for new marketing hooks which will help capture this audience.

USING AWARDS

As was discussed in the previous section of this book (Markets and Festivals), festival awards can be extremely useful tools when designing the campaign for certain types of film, particularly arthouse pictures. An award from a festival is often a sign that the film represents a particularly fine example of its genre, especially if the award is from a festival devoted to a specific genre of film.[11] The seal of approval by a prestigious international jury will provide a tangible hook for the distributor in building the advertising and publicity campaign.

If the distributor makes effective use of such marketing hooks, media interest in the film will increase, which will in turn serve substantially to raise awareness of the title among its target audience. The distributor may mention the award for a film on the poster, in the trailer campaign or in other advertising materials. In some cases, the distinctive logo of a festival award may be incorporated into the artwork for the film.

The most important awards, in terms of the free publicity they generate, are the top prizes in Cannes (including the Camera d'Or for best first film), Venice and Berlin. But the impact of such awards on cinema admissions is always difficult to predict, as the performance of a given film may be affected by other variables.[12]

In the case of mainstream films, the awards – known as Oscars – given by the Academy of Motion Picture Arts and Sciences (AMPAS) in the last week of March, can have an enormous impact on the performance of a film, both in terms of theatrical release and on video. There will be extremely comprehensive

11 Festivals devoted to particular genres of film would include the festival of Vevey in Switzerland, held in August, which concentrates on comedy films.

12 See the section on the Cannes Film Festival p.109.

> " **A picture may often benefit simply from being nominated for an award, since a nomination does a great deal to raise the public profile of a film.** "

media coverage of Oscar nominees, and especially the eventual winners.[13] The Oscar awarded for Best Foreign Language Film can also help the performance of arthouse films.[14] The Golden Globes, awarded in January by the Hollywood Foreign Press Association, may also have some impact in raising the profile of a picture.

A picture may often benefit simply from being nominated for an award, since a nomination does a great deal to raise the public profile of a film. The British film The Crying Game more than doubled its weekend gross at the UK box office after it was nominated for six Oscars in 1993.

As will be discussed below (see Calendar of major events p.72/73), distributors will often plan to release films that may be potential nominees for an award to coincide with the unveiling of the nominations, so as to benefit from the attendant publicity.

EXPLOITING PERFORMANCE IN OTHER TERRITORIES

For certain European films, the performance of the film in a specific territory can be influenced by its success in its country of origin, but this is usually only applicable where the two territories share the same language. For example, if a French-language film is successful at the box office, this will generate coverage in the French media, with beneficial effects in neighbouring territories such as French-speaking Belgium and French-speaking Switzerland, which are also penetrated by French television and newspapers. Widespread media coverage of a successful German language film in Germany itself, will help raise the profile of the film in German-speaking Switzerland and in Austria.

From the viewpoint of the distributor handling a film which has already achieved success in other territories, it is the media coverage devoted to the film that will be the main benefit of such success at the foreign box office, because of increased audience awareness of the picture.

Wherever appropriate, a distributor will play up the success of the film abroad when approaching the media to try to secure editorial coverage. Although the distributor has little, if any,

---

13 "Conventional wisdom is that a best picture Oscar is worth an additional $20-35 million at the box office... Another much vaunted industry tenet contends that a best picture Oscar boosts video revenues by some 15% worldwide." Variety, February 22nd, 1993.

---

14 Recent winners of this Oscar include the French picture Indochine (1993), and the Italian film Mediterraneo (1992).

KEY MARKETING ELEMENTS

STARS • The names of the stars. Crucial selling point for most mainstream and some arthouse films.

DIRECTOR • The name of the director. Can be important in helping to create audience appeal, notably in arthouse pictures.

GENRE • The genre and story ingredients. Genre of the film is often the first marketing hook, making the audience aware of the type of film it can expect.

AWARDS • Awards won at significant international film festivals. Big awards can raise awareness of the project among the press and its target audience.

BOX OFFICE • Box-office performance in other territories. Helpful only if relevant media have been made aware.

influence over such foreign coverage, the resulting exposure will be enormously helpful when approaching national journalists since they are much more likely to be aware of the picture. This will make it considerably easier to generate publicity for the film. In certain cases, the national distributor may also wish to incorporate quotes from foreign media into the publicity material for the film, although some European countries such as France seldom use quotes in this way.

For many European distributors, a strong performance by a film at the US box office will be a particularly valuable element in planning their marketing campaign for a film. However, this is usually only applicable to US films. This is because it is rare for non-US films to be released in that market prior to release in their country of origin and, in any case, the US box office tends to be dominated by indigenous films. For most European films, the US release will tend to follow after they have been released in Europe.

Films which are successful in the US will inevitably attract considerable attention in the media and this will filter through to Europe, either through coverage in US publications distributed abroad or as a result of the fact that many European publications devote considerable space to Hollywood films and their stars.

These are some of the key elements that the distributor will use in the construction of a marketing campaign for a film. It is now time to turn and examine the way in which the distributor identifies the target audience for a film.

WHAT IS THE TARGET AUDIENCE FOR A FILM?

Before the distributor starts to plan and implement the marketing campaign for a film, it is vital to be able to identify its target audience. The distributor will also seek to establish whether it is possible to widen the appeal of the film beyond its immediate target audience.

The factors that will be taken into account in defining the target audience are as follows: age, gender and income level of cinema goers. For every film that they release, the distributors must determine which segment of the population they are trying to reach, and these categories will help pinpoint that audience.

In broad terms, there four main groups of cinema goers in Europe. The groups, in terms of age profile, are:

- Children aged 7-14 years

- Young adults aged 15-24 years

- Adults aged 25-34 years

- Adults aged over 35

The core group of cinema goers in Europe are young adults between 14-24. Many members of this demographic group go to the cinema at least once a month. They also tend to be highly responsive to trends, and film marketing campaigns can often exploit this desire to identify with certain fashions. In many countries, the adult audience goes to the cinema, on average, less than just once a year. The distributor will set out to identify the target audience of the film on the basis of the film's ingredients, such as subject matter, genre and the stars featured in the film. Certain types of genre, such as romance, will tend to appeal more to women, while action-adventure is a more male-oriented genre. There will also be certain stars who will have a predominantly male following, while others will appeal primarily to females.

The knowledge of which elements are likely to appeal to which segments of the population will be guided in part by the past track record of films in a similar genre or which featured particular stars. But as has been repeatedly emphasised, because every film is a unique entity, it will never be sufficient to assume that, for example, just because a certain title featuring a certain star appealed strongly to women between 15-20, that the same will apply to the next feature in which that star appears.

In many cases, the distributor will seek to identify the primary audience for a film, together with a *secondary* audience, which will help broaden the appeal of the film.

Cinema audience composition by age in 6 EC countries (1990)
(ages in italic)

France	*15 ———— 24* **34.8%**	*25 - 34* **20.8%**	*35 ———— 49* **25.4%**		*50+* **19%**
Italy	*14 ———— 24* **49.6%**	*25 - 34* **26.5%**	*35 - 44* **11.9%**		*45+* **12%**
UK	*15 ———— 24* **61.4%**	*25 - 34* **23.3%**	*35 - 44* **9.3%**		*45+* **6%**
Belgium	*15 - 19* **28.2%**	*20 -24* **19.5%**	*25 - 34* **25.6%**	*35 - 44* **14%**	*45+* **12.7%**
Spain	*14 - 19* **32.4%**	*20 - 24* **24.6%**	*25 - 34* **26.9%**	*35 - 44* **9.5%**	*45+* **6.6%**
Germany	*14 - 19* **26%**	*20 - 24* **49%**	*25 ———— 39* **14%**	*40 - 49* **7%**	*50+* **4%**

source : Screen Digest/authors' research

The chart above shows that 14-24 year olds are the most avid cinema goers. The secondary audience for films are the 25-34 year olds in most territories except in France where the 35-49 year olds represent a higher percentage.

DETERMINING THE DATE AND PATTERN OF RELEASE FOR A FILM

After the distributor has identified the target audience for a film and set a P&A budget, three key factors must be considered: when should the film be released, with what number of prints and in which cinemas?

Before examining the optimum release dates and typical release patterns in Europe, it is first necessary to explore the relationship between the distributor and the exhibitor.

TARGETING THE EXHIBITOR

If the picture is to reach the paying public, the distributor must first licence the film to the exhibitor. The relationship is essentially that of supplier to retailer. But with power increasingly concentrated in the cinema circuits, the negotiating muscle of independent distributors has been eroded in some European territories (especially in France and Italy).

In most instances the distributor will show an exhibitor a film prior to the exhibitor deciding to licence it. However, in some instances, the exhibitor may have to licence the film without seeing it, particularly in the case of large US films which are booked into cinema circuits well ahead of release.[15] If the exhibitor likes the film, a decision is jointly made with the distributor as to when the film will open, how many prints will go out and how the release will subsequently develop.

They will also jointly determine the *percentage deal* indicating the split of gross receipts between the distributor and the exhibitor and other parties as well as, in some cases, the length of run. The percentage the exhibitor pays to the distributor, which is known as the *net rental*, or the distributor's *gross receipts*, is negotiable and varies from country to country. It ranges from a low of 30% of the box-office rentals to a high of 70%, with a typical 50/50 split on the first net rentals.[16]

15 As explained in Section Six, it is the task of the booker to acquire and book films for a cinema circuit.

16 See also Section Six: Exhibition in Europe.

" **With power increasingly concentrated in the cinema circuits, the negotiating muscle of independent distributors has been eroded in some European territories.** "

The distributor deals with many types of exhibitor ranging from large cinema circuits controlling hundreds of screens to small independent operators who own only one cinema. Depending on the nature of the particular film they are handling, distributors will approach specific types of exhibitor, felt to be best suited to the title. Targeting the right cinema for a particular film is part of the marketing strategy. A distributor has to know the seating capacity of the cinema and the types of audience which it usually attracts. Identifying the audience profile of a cinema will be particularly important in the case of specialised films which are targeted at niche audiences.

Mainstream pictures will predominantly be booked into the major cinema chains, while arthouse pictures will tend to be targeted at independent houses. For films which are felt to have cross-over potential, both types of cinema may be used.

Certain cinemas will create an identity so that they are inexorably associated with arthouse films. This will be done not only through the programming strategy but also by installing facilities such as coffee bars or a bookshop which are likely to appeal to an arthouse audience. Moreover, just as there are cross-over films so there are cross-over cinemas, where many of the regular customers will pay to see arthouse films as well as certain mainstream pictures, with quality production values.

Some arthouse cinemas have adapted their facilities to the needs of the audience, and devote 50-60% of their screen time to small, quality European films, with the rest of the time devoted to more mainstream releases. To support the efforts made by these distributors to show European films, the MEDIA programme has created the Europa Cinémas initiative.

The development of the multiplex cinema across much of Europe has also increased the possibilities for flexible programming within a single cinema complex.[17]

BOOKING For all types of film it is vital for the distributor to book the screens as far as possible in advance to allow time to implement an effective marketing plan. For mainstream films, distributors can generally book their dates and cinemas from three to six months in advance. In some territories – Greece for example – bookings

17 See Section Six: Exhibition in Europe for more information on how different types of cinema position themselves in the market.

are made on a yearly basis. Potential blockbusters with names, bought on script, can also be booked a year in advance. These films will include European titles as long as they are made for a large audience and have commercial potential.

In some cases, the dates are still subject to modification, as exhibitors may decide to extend the run of a film that is performing particularly well. Such a film is known as a **hold-over**. As a result the release of subsequent films may be put back, which may force the distributor to change aspects of the marketing campaign – like the timing of advertisements in newspapers or magazines – at very short notice.

Distributors of specialised films also prefer to book pictures into the exhibition schedule as far ahead of the release as possible. It is important to secure a release date in good time since many magazines which will provide important editorial coverage of specialised titles may have a three-month gap between their press deadline and their publication date, a period which is known as the **lead time**.

However, such distributors often face the problem of convincing the exhibitor of the relative commercial value of a specialised film. In many cases, the exhibitor will only be prepared to commit to the film after having seen it. The distributor may also wish to wait until the title has received exposure – for instance through a film festival which provides press attention – before booking it or may hold back until the film has achieved box-office success in its country of origin.

Most specialised films are booked into the cinema from two to five months ahead of release. Arthouse cinemas tend to have a more rigid booking policy so that a film will be booked in for a four- or five-week run, and so long as the film grosses more than the **house nut** – the weekly overhead costs of the cinema – it will complete its run. In the case of foreign-language films, the distributor will need to ensure in advance that a subtitled or dubbed print will be delivered in time for the proposed release.

> " For all types of film it is vital for the distributor to book the screens as far as possible in advance to allow time to implement an effective marketing plan. "

So when booking films, and particularly the more specialised titles, it is necessary for distributors constantly to pressure the exhibitors in order to convince them of their value, and thus to secure strong release dates. The distributor will strive at all times to cultivate the best possible personal relationships in the service of obtaining these dates.

The interests of an exhibitor and distributor are rather different, however, and this can lead to conflict particularly in the case of pictures which do not perform as strongly as expected. If a film is significantly under-performing the exhibitor will want to pull it off the screens as quickly as possible, while the distributor will want to recover as much of the costs of the P&A campaign as possible through extending the run.

Distributors who also have interests in exhibition, such as Gaumont/UGC in France, Penta in Italy and even some smaller companies such as Lauren Films in Spain, are in a stronger position than most of their rivals when it comes to booking films, since they have a much greater level of control over the playdates.[18] On occasion this can create problems for others, since some distributors/exhibitors may be tempted to give their own films preferential treatment at the expense of films acquired from other parties.

To have more power vis-à-vis exhibitors and to guarantee playdates and cinemas, some independent distributors have joined forces with the US majors' arms. They supervise the distribution of the independents' films – the booking of cinemas and the collection of film rental revenues – while the distributor supervises the marketing. For example BIM Distribuzione has an agreement with Columbia Tri-Star in Italy, and Iberoamericana is aligned with UIP in Spain.

SELECTING THE DATE OF RELEASE

Those responsible for planning the release date and pattern can play a pivotal role in determining the box-office fate of a film. Their decisions, along with the decisions of those who create the advertising and publicity campaign, may have considerable impact on a film's performance. If they make a misjudgment about the best date of release or the required number of prints, even the strongest title can see its box-office performance suffer heavily.

The day of the week on which a film opens is usually determined by the accepted practice within a particular country. As shown in the accompanying chart, the day varies from country to country. However, the positioning of a particular film may sometimes be helped by the choice of an alternative opening day. For example, Ridley Scott's 1492, Christopher Columbus, opened in France on a Monday instead of a Wednesday, because the date (October 12th) coincided with the anniversary of the discovery of America.

---

18 See Section Six: Exhibition in Europe.

Change over days for the release of films in EC countries

The chart right indicates that Friday is the most common change over day. There is no fixed change over day in Italy, but Tuesday is the most common day.

Belgium,
France

Germany,
Netherlands

Denmark,
Greece, Ireland,
Luxembourg,
Portugal, UK

Three key factors influence the decision as to when to open a film:

TIME OF YEAR

The time of year when a film is to open must be considered very carefully, bearing in mind the rhythm of cinema going over the year. The frequency of cinema going in Europe is subject to strong seasonal fluctuations – linked to the weather and to holiday periods (see chart on next page). The pattern of cinema going over the year may be broken down into three distinct periods:

- **September to December**
  Cinema going is at its peak and is especially high over the Christmas holiday period, when admissions may reach as much as 30% above average, with the exception of the UK which is much more irregular. During the holiday period, cinema going is a family event with the result that films aimed at children or young teenagers perform particularly strongly.

- **January to April**
  Admissions remain strong, usually peaking over the Easter holiday. In Mediterranean countries admissions may start to fall as early as April, as with the increase in temperature people turn to outdoor leisure pursuits.

- **May to August**
  This is usually considered the time of the year when the independent distributor releasing a film faces the highest risks (particularly in the Mediterranean countries) as the level of attendances can be

Seasonality of admissions in the key EC countries (Index: average month = 100)

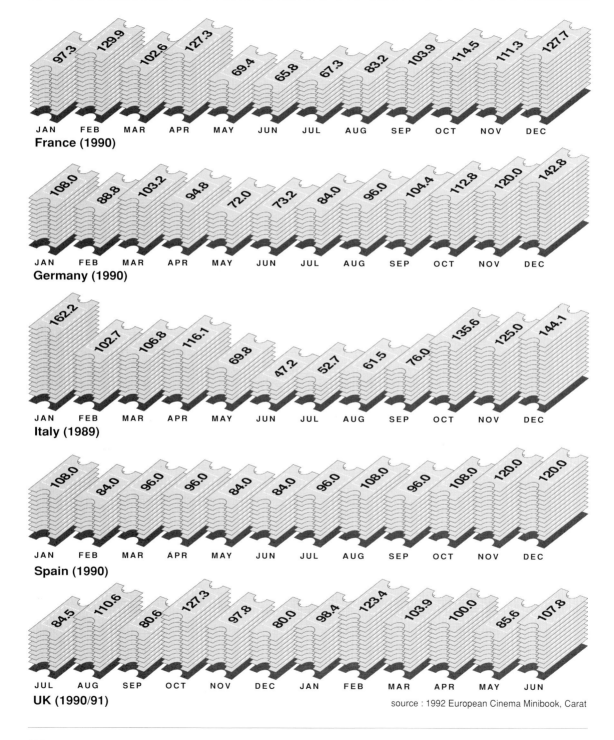

France (1990)

JAN 97.3 · FEB 129.9 · MAR 102.6 · APR 127.3 · MAY 69.4 · JUN 65.8 · JUL 67.3 · AUG 83.2 · SEP 103.9 · OCT 114.5 · NOV 111.3 · DEC 127.7

Germany (1990)

JAN 108.0 · FEB 88.8 · MAR 103.2 · APR 94.8 · MAY 72.0 · JUN 73.2 · JUL 84.0 · AUG 96.0 · SEP 104.4 · OCT 112.8 · NOV 120.0 · DEC 142.8

Italy (1989)

JAN 162.2 · FEB 102.7 · MAR 106.8 · APR 116.1 · MAY 69.8 · JUN 47.2 · JUL 52.7 · AUG 61.5 · SEP 76.0 · OCT 135.6 · NOV 125.0 · DEC 144.1

Spain (1990)

JAN 108.0 · FEB 84.0 · MAR 96.0 · APR 96.0 · MAY 84.0 · JUN 84.0 · JUL 96.0 · AUG 108.0 · SEP 96.0 · OCT 108.0 · NOV 120.0 · DEC 120.0

UK (1990/91)

JUL 84.5 · AUG 110.6 · SEP 80.6 · OCT 127.3 · NOV 97.8 · DEC 80.0 · JAN 98.4 · FEB 123.4 · MAR 103.9 · APR 100.0 · MAY 85.6 · JUN 107.8

source : 1992 European Cinema Minibook, Carat

heavily affected by the weather. Traditionally, it is large Hollywood films released by the US majors which have dominated the European box office during this period. Since such films often ride on the back of the vast publicity campaigns which accompanied their release just a few weeks before in the US, fluctuations in the weather tend to have far less impact on their box-office performance in Europe.[19]

Until the late 1980s, few European distributors were prepared to open potentially strong films during this period. But as the multiplex cinema has spread across Europe, and as exhibitors have introduced air-conditioning into many older cinemas, the weather has become less of a factor and independent distributors are prepared to open a much wider range of pictures during this period. Promotional initiatives such as the Fête du Cinéma, held in France in late June, and the Festa del Cinema in Italy in May/June have also helped boost attendances in both countries compared with earlier admissions during the same period.[20]

COMPETITION FROM OTHER TITLES

The optimum opening dates for a film will also be the most heavily booked dates. Distributors generally know in advance that their competitors will also play at the same time; they can either decide to compete head to head or choose another date to open. Even varying a release by a single week can make a considerable difference to the performance of a film.

This is particularly true in the case of specialised titles which are likely to be heavily dependent on reviews as an opinion-forming tool. In such cases, the distributor will try to ensure that the film is the strongest release in a particular week, since this will help the picture secure a prominent position when a critic comes to review the week's releases.

Generally, mainstream commercial films can be released at any time during the year, although they tend to monopolise the screens over holiday periods. Arthouse films need a longer run to increase word of mouth, so it is often best for them to open in less competitive times of the year – outside the holiday periods, for example.

19 In the US the summer release period is one of the strongest periods for releasing films, particularly those aimed at the teenage market.

20 In 1993, admissions during the week of the Fête du Cinéma (27-29th June) in France were 47.3% higher than in the same week in 1992 when the Fête was held over just one day. In Italy the Festa del Cinema, held in the last week of May and the first week of June 1992, produced a 68.6% rise in admissions against the same (ordinary) period a year earlier.

> " **The skilful use of counter-programming by independent distributors will enable them to offer a serious challenge to films with a much larger marketing budget.** "

Genre is another factor to be considered when choosing the opening date. If there are three strong action films and thrillers on release, a smaller romantic movie, released simultaneously, will offer the audience an alternative. Or it may be fruitful to open an arthouse film during the school holidays so that it offers an alternative to the larger number of films aimed at children. Such a strategy is known as *counter-programming*.

As an example of counter-programming, Jan Verheyen, managing director of Belgian distribution company Independent, cites the comedy Nobody's Perfect. The company believed that the film could break out from its target audience and become a cross-over title. "We invested in a widespread advertising campaign, with plenty of trailers, and billboard advertising," he says. The film was opened against the Warner Brothers blockbuster Batman, and performed very strongly because, Verheyen believes, it offered a definite alternative to the US title.

The skilful use of counter-programming by independent distributors will enable them to offer a serious challenge to films with a much larger marketing budget.

USING KEY DATES IN THE FILM CALENDAR

The positioning of films around the Oscars and, to a lesser degree, film festivals, can have a significant impact on box-office performance. If a film wins or is even just nominated for an Oscar, it can significantly increase the box-office gross of the title. Festivals are generally used as platforms for arthouse films that will benefit from the media coverage and word of mouth generated.

- **The Oscars**
  European distributors with films they feel are potential Oscar nominees will often try to hold back the release dates until the nominations are unveiled in mid-February. In this way, the film will open just as the nominations are announced, and if the film is nominated, it should receive considerable publicity in the run-up to the event itself in late March.

  This strategy is something of a gamble, however, since if the film is not nominated the distributor may not be able to secure cinemas as the film will have lost one of its main marketing hooks – the nomination itself. Even if a cinema is secured, the distributor will then be competing with films that have been selected.

Alternatively, the distributor may release the film on a relatively small scale at an earlier date, broadening the release as the nominations are unveiled. In this way, the distributor will maximise the potential box office of the title.

The US majors are particularly attuned to the importance of the Oscars, as many of the pictures that they handle will be among those submitted for Oscar nominations. "A possible Oscar nominee will be slotted in for release during February or March," says Hy Smith, senior vice president of marketing for UIP.

The award of an Oscar can add between 10-50% to a film's box-office gross, depending on the country, and as a result distributors are often keen to re-release the winners, as soon after the ceremony as possible. For example, when The Silence of the Lambs was re-released in Italy it grossed more than it did during its first run, even though it was already available on video.[21]

The nominees for Best Foreign Film Oscar will already have opened in most European territories prior to the ceremony, and the Academy Award nomination will usually have little impact. For example, the Oscar for Journey of Hope did not have any box-office impact in Europe. However, the re-release of an Oscar winner in its own country can be extremely lucrative; Mediterraneo, re-released in Italy, almost doubled its first-run revenues after it won the Best Foreign Film award.

The Oscars are excellent promotional tools that create considerable public awareness but their effect on European box-office receipts varies widely.

- ### The Cannes Film Festival
  The Cannes Film Festival is the most important international film festival, with around 3500 accredited journalists covering both the festival and the market. The effects of the press reaction to a film can extend far beyond the event itself and the impact of reviews at Cannes frequently offer a stark demonstration of the power of the media.

  With such extensive free publicity surrounding the screening of a film at the event itself, distributors are often tempted to exploit the publicity generated by the film at the festival, by launching the film at the same time in its home territory. The release date can be set for a time during the festival, preferably before the awards ceremony, or before the screening of the film.[22]

21 See Section Four: Markets and Festivals for more details of the impact of the Oscars.

22 Films cannot be entered for the official competition at Cannes if they have been released outside their national territory.

Because of the intensity of the attention focused on Cannes, and the fact that the critics view an enormous number of films within a very short space of time there, the media reaction to films often swings between the extremes of extravagant praise and extreme hostility. The domestic box-office performance of a film will often benefit from the impact of a favourable response at Cannes. Equally, however, poor reviews from Cannes can often destroy the box-office potential of a picture. This is especially true for French films, since the French media devotes considerable attention to the event.

For a small film that is entirely dependent on reviews, an excellent response at Cannes can be enormously beneficial. This was the case for the Italian film Il Ladro di Bambini which, while featuring no stars, provoked a very positive response at Cannes and was awarded the Grand Prix du Jury in 1992. The enthusiastic reaction at Cannes did much to boost the subsequent box office of the film in Italy.

In many cases, the press reaction at Cannes can have a more significant effect on the fate of a film than the official awards. Once again, however, there are no firm rules governing this relationship, as New Zealander Jane Campion's The Piano, 1993 co-winner of Cannes' most prestigious prize the Palme d'Or, did achieve a significant performance in box office in France, partly as a result of receiving the prize. On the other hand, the Palme d'Or had little impact on the international box-office revenues of the Swedish film The Best Intentions, which won in 1992.

> **" Winning an award at a prominent festival does provide a marketing hook which the distributor can use when negotiating with the exhibitor for screens and release dates. "**

Winning an award at a prominent festival, however, does provide a marketing hook which the distributor can use when negotiating with the exhibitor for screens and release dates.

If a film is chosen as part of the official selection at Cannes this will give it a relatively high profile at the festival, which may filter back to the media in other territories. In many cases, the film will receive coverage in the arts pages of quality newspapers which often set aside considerable space for editorial on Cannes. Even if a film is chosen to be screened outside official competition (when it may still receive a gala screening) or in a sidebar event such as the Director's Fortnight it may still benefit from the effects of the media spotlight.

The Berlin festival in February and the Venice festival, held in September, are also widely covered by the media, and the publicity accorded to a film as a result of media coverage at one of these festivals can also be very helpful to a distributor launching a picture in a given territory. Hundreds of other local film festivals are held in Europe every year and they are often used by distributors to position their film in the local market and to stage special gala premieres.

Because the media that cover these festivals tend to constitute a close-knit community among which opinions travel quickly, even a small film on the festival circuit may rapidly be surrounded by a favourable "buzz". This may percolate through the media in many territories, with immediate benefit for the box office of the film when it is finally released within a particular country.

RELEASE PATTERN

The pattern of release for a film can be as crucial as the date of release in determining the box-office success of a film. Factors which the distributor will assess when considering the release pattern are the number of prints in which the film should be released, the specific cinemas in which the film will be released, and the towns and cities where the film will play.

There are two patterns of types of release:

DAY AND DATE RELEASE

For a day and date release, a distributor will release a film on the same day throughout the country, generally with the maximum number of prints. A *wide-opening* release also utilises the maximum number of prints, although release dates are staggered, starting with key cities. Both techniques are used for mainstream commercial pictures, and are designed to create the maximum awareness possible during the opening week or weekend of release and to take advantage of the large advertising spend timed to coincide with the opening date.

If a film does not open well, it is usually very difficult for it to recover. The day and date release will be backed up by an extensive advertising and publicity campaign. The day and date release, however, often shortens the life of a film, as there is usually limited demand for each film, and it therefore accelerates the rotation of films on screen.

A successful day and date release should ensure the relatively quick passage of substantial revenues from exhibitor to producer. A failure, however, can be disastrous for the distributor, since it can often shorten the life of a film and the costs of the P&A budget will be very high. So for this type of release, the stakes are high, especially for the independent distributor. On films which are expected to perform poorly, however, a day and date release can be advantageous since it can enable such films to gross more in their first week – before negative word of mouth starts to circulate among the potential audience.

"A strong opening is essential to sustain the life of a movie, as it's in the first week of opening that the exhibitor will decide to keep a film or not," says Duncan Clark, executive vice-president of international marketing at Columbia Tri-Star Film Distributors International.

The scale of a day and date release differs according to the type of film and marketplace. A blockbuster from a US major can go out with as many as 600 prints in Germany, 400 in France, and 100 in Spain. Large independent distributors can also afford similar saturation releases for mainstream films featuring major stars, although the cost of prints may sometimes act as a deterrent.

PLATFORM RELEASE

The platform release is often used for specialised films that need a long run to develop word of mouth. In a platform release, the number of initial prints is limited. In many ways, such a release is much harder to plan than that for a mainstream film. It is in handling the specialised releases that the targeting of the audience can be particularly tricky. In these cases creativity and an understanding of the potential audience can be as important as the amount of money available.

In the case of a platform release, it is vital to target properly the city where the film will open. There is a greater level of awareness of films in capital cities, where a greater number of cinemas means a greater diversity in programming, and adult audiences have increased access to quality films. There is also a higher level of disposable income available for cinema going in these cities.

A mainstream commercial film can be platformed in a cinema in the capital city of a given country during its first week of release, or even for several weeks, in the hope that coverage from the media which tends to be concentrated in such cities will boost the profile of the film before it goes nationwide. For instance, in its first week of release Fried Green Tomatoes was released by Rank at the Odeon Haymarket in London only, and in the second week it was released with 124 prints in 20 key cities and this was later widened to 160 prints.

In Italy, Roberto Cimpanelli, chief executive officer with the distribution company Life International, released Dances With

Wolves with 15 prints to judge initial reaction, later widening the release to 80 prints, and eventually to 300 prints.

A more specialised film can be platformed with one print in an exclusive run, or with several prints at a small number of prestige houses such as, for example, the Curzon Mayfair, the Gate and the Lumière cinemas in London. If a film is shown only in one cinema, the distributor is effectively emphasising the exclusivity of the picture. Platforming the film in several cinemas conveys to the audience the notion that the film is a quality picture, but also amortises the advertising and public relations expenditure across a number of screens.

In the UK, most specialised or arthouse films open in London, followed by release in the provinces anywhere from two to six weeks later. In Spain, such pictures would typically open in Madrid and Barcelona, before being released in other cities. In Italy a platform release will often open in Rome and Milan, and a few weeks later the release will be widened to include such cities as Florence, Bologna and Naples. In Germany, the consensus is that there are seven key cities: Berlin, Hamburg, Munich, Frankfurt, Düsseldorf, Stuttgart and Cologne. The key cities in Europe are shown in the accompanying chart.

Judging the optimum strategy for a platform release requires the distributor to balance the most effective way of targeting the audience against cost. It is wise not to overspend at the beginning of a campaign for a platform release, since it is important to maintain interest on the part of the public and slowly build an audience through *release advertising*, often using quotes from favourable reviews.

The distributor must spend sufficient money for the various elements of the marketing campaign – advertising, publicity and promotion – to have an impact. One advertisement or interview is not enough to create awareness let alone want to see, as the message must be reinforced over a period of several weeks. This is where the media will play a major role. However, the sheer costs of P&A can also make it uneconomic to open with a very small number of prints. Balancing the different components of the advertising spend is critical to the bottom line.

Box-office receipts in London and Paris, for example, are a useful indication of how a film will perform in the provinces. In other European countries there tend to be several key cities which act as an indicator for the likely level of overall box office within a specific territory. After opening in these key cities a film will subsequently be released to a second wave of smaller cities, and then to a third wave of minor cities and towns.

Key European cities for the release of films

Belgium BRUSSELS, LIEGE, ANTWERP, GHENT

Denmark COPENHAGEN, AARHUS

France PARIS, MARSEILLE, BORDEAUX, TOULOUSE, METZ, LILLE, ROUEN, NANCY, NICE, LYON, STRASBOURG, GRENOBLE

Germany BERLIN, COLOGNE, HAMBURG, MUNICH, FRANKFURT, DUSSELDORF, STUTTGART, DRESDEN, LEIPZIG, ERFURT

Greece ATHENS, SALONICA, PATRAS

Ireland DUBLIN, CORK

Italy ROME, MILAN, FLORENCE, BOLOGNA, NAPLES, PADUA, BARI, CALGARI, CATANIA

Luxembourg LUXEMBOURG

Netherlands AMSTERDAM, ROTTERDAM, THE HAGUE, UTRECHT

Portugal LISBON, OPORTO

Spain MADRID, BARCELONA, SEVILLE, BILBAO, VALENCIA, ZARAGOZA

UK LONDON, EDINBURGH, GLASGOW, NEWCASTLE, MANCHESTER, BRIGHTON, LIVERPOOL, BIRMINGHAM, CARDIFF, OXFORD, SOUTHAMPTON, CAMBRIDGE, BRISTOL, LEEDS, SHEFFIELD, NOTTINGHAM

While the playdate and release pattern are set, the tools which will be used to position the film for its target audience are being developed. Once definite dates are in place, a strategy for the use of these tools will be put in place. It is time to consider how this strategy is developed.

KEY POINTS OF RELEASE STRATEGY

TARGETING THE EXHIBITOR

For all types of film it is vital for the distributor to book the screens as far as possible in advance to allow time to implement an effective marketing plan. For mainstream films, distributors can generally book their dates and cinemas from three to six months in advance. Distributors of more specialised films will usually decide the release date and attempt to book the cinemas from two to five months in advance.

DETERMINING THE DATE OF RELEASE

Timing

The choice of date can have considerable impact on the box-office success of a film. Admissions are highest during holiday periods, especially Christmas. During the summer, admissions can be significantly affected by the weather.

Competition

The competition from titles opening the same day is to be seriously analysed when choosing a release date. Arthouse distributors should try to ensure that their films are in a strong position compared with other titles in order to get effective media coverage.

Using key dates in the film calendar

The positioning of films around major film festivals like Cannes, or major awards like the Oscars, can generate a considerable amount of free publicity.

RELEASE PATTERN

The pattern of release for a film can be as crucial as the date of release in determining the box-office success of a film.

Day and date release

For a day and date release, or wide-opening release, a distributor will release a film on the same day throughout the country with the maximum number of prints.

Platform release

The platform release is often used for specialised films that need a long run to develop word of mouth. It is vital to target cinemas in the city or cities where the film will open and select a release date which will provide maximum editorial and critical exposure.

THE PRINTS AND ADVERTISING BUDGET

Determining the most effective P&A budget for a film is one of the most critical parts of the marketing process, since without an adequate budget the likelihood of the film reaching its target audience is greatly reduced. The P&A budget of a film comprises the cost of prints, advertising, publicity and promotion. In the US, it may also include the cost of market research but, as discussed below, independent distributors in Europe rarely use this tool.

HOW THE P&A BUDGET BREAKS DOWN

The main items of expenditure which constitute the P&A budget are:

PRINT COSTS INCLUDING:

- Subtitling or dubbing, if the film is in a foreign language and is not going to be shown in the original version.

- Accessing or buying an inter-negative, from which to make up the required number of prints.

- Production of the prints themselves, known as feature prints, plus duplication of any trailer prints.

- Shipping prints and duty payable on materials imported from abroad.

- Costs sometimes incurred because of the necessity of re-cutting to meet censorship requirements.

ADVERTISING COSTS INCLUDING:

- Designing and printing posters for display in the cinema and on advertising hoardings.

- Creating trailers, which will run prior to the film's release.

- Advertising space in newspapers and magazines.

- Advertising spots on radio.

- Advertising time on television.

- Advertising within cinemas.

- Outdoor advertising (on billboards, buses and trains as well as flyposting).

PUBLICITY COSTS INCLUDING:

- Stills (black-and-white) for distribution to media.

- Transparencies (colour) for distribution to media.

- Electronic press kits (EPKs) for television and radio.

- Other press kits for printed media.

- One-sheets (these are the industry-norm posters, measuring 1016mm x 685mm) for distribution to media and/or general public.

- Press screenings of a film organised for the media in advance of its release for the purpose of reviews and to spread awareness of the film.

- Press attaché, hired to secure media coverage of the film.

- Special stills – buying in outside stills of stars and/or director or doing special photo shoots.

PROMOTIONAL COSTS INCLUDING:

- Merchandising, such as the production of toys or free gifts to promote the film.

- Tie-ins, such as competitions arranged in conjunction with radio stations or retail outlets.

- Talker screenings, which are set up in advance of the official release, designed to spread awareness of the film, largely through word of mouth.

THEATRICAL P&A BUDGET

This is a typical P&A budget form that an international sales agent or producer would request their distributor to complete in order to analyse not only how much is being spent on the release of the film, but how it is being spent. There is much more to releasing a film than simply asking how much is being spent and how many prints the film is being released with. Cost-effective marketing by distributors is often the difference between a film which returns a profit not only to themselves, but to the sales agent and then eventually to the producer and/or financiers. Careless overspending or tracking of P&A spends can negate any such financial return.

Title of film
Local title if different from above
Proposed release date
Number of prints/Cities for opening release   /
Number of prints/Cities for continuation release   /
Number of trailers
Projected gross box office   US$
Projected net rentals   US$

Report summary
Proposed P&A budget (A+B)   US$
Proposed production & misc budget (C+D+E)   US$

TOTAL RELEASING BUDGET   US$

Date submitted:

(A) Advertising
1 Newspapers - Advance
            - Opening week
2 Magazines - Advance
            - Opening week
3 Specialised press
4 Radio
5 Cinema screen
6 Outdoor sites/Bus/Metro, bus shelters
   Billboard/Poster sites

7 Other

Total Advertising Spend   US$

(B) Publicity

1 Promotions

2 Standees

3 Front of house stills/
   Theatre displays

4 Outside publicity

5 Stills/press kits

6 Talker screenings/Trade shows

7 Tie-ins, merchandising

8 Direct mail

9 Previews, premiere/Receptions

10 Flyposting

11 Star tours

Total publicity spend   US$

TOTAL ADVERTISING/PUBLICITY   US$

(C) Ad/Pub production costs

1 Poster art (design)

2 Printing of posters

3 Press books

4 Stills

5 TV/Radio spots

6 Creation/Adaptation of trailer

7 Other producton costs

Total Ad/Pub costs   US$

(D) Print & Trailer production costs

1 Feature inter-negative

2 Trailer inter-negative

3 No. of feature prints   at   each

5 Subtitling costs

6 Dubbing costs

7 Shipping costs

Total print production costs   US$

(E) Miscellaneous

1 Research/Test screenings

2 Other

Total other costs   US$

**TOTAL AD/PUB, PRINT, PRODUCTION
& MISC COSTS**   US$

The P&A budget is often contractually fixed with the distributor and sales agent or producer, with a specified minimum and maximum spend. The costs are generally borne by the distributor. Once the film is released, and subject to the sales agreement with the producer or sales representative, the P&A costs will be deducted before the producers' share is calculated, but after the distributor has taken a commission fee and deducted costs.[23]

This type of deal, known as **cost off the top** (COT), is most common when the distributor has paid an up-front minimum guarantee to the sales agent, for the right to distribute the film in a certain territory for a specified length of time.[24]

If a minimum guarantee has not been advanced, the distributor will usually participate in the first receipts alongside the producer, after the exhibitor's share has been deducted. In this type of deal – a **gross deal** – the distributor will take a much higher percentage – up to 70-80% of the total – because P&A costs have to be recouped from these receipts. Once the P&A is recouped by the distributor the percentage split of receipts between the producer and the distributor will usually be set at 50/50.

In many cases, the amount spent on P&A in a particular territory may equal the minimum guarantee for the film. If, for example, the minimum guarantee put up by a UK distributor for a film is $100,000 (ECU90,000), this will often mean that the same amount of money will be spent on P&A. The film would then have to generate between $300,000-400,000 (ECU270,000-360,000) gross at the box office (allowing for deductions including Value Added Tax (VAT), and the exhibitor's share) for the distributor to break even.[25] Assuming that the picture grosses this amount, the 25% remitted to the distributor is the net rental.

After the distributor has taken a share of the net rentals, the remainder will be split between the sales agent and the producer, according to a previously-agreed formula which will usually vary picture by picture.

CALCULATING P&A COSTS

The marketing budget for a film is usually calculated in terms of the projected box office of the film, and its likely performance in ancillary media. As has been stressed above, it is the marketing of

23 See Section Six: Exhibition in Europe, Net Rental for an explanation of how the exhibitors share of the box office is calculated.

24 See Section Three: International Sales.

25 Value Added Tax is not charged on cinema tickets in every European country.

a film for its cinema release which will create the greatest impact, and thus the theatrical campaign will also be important in helping its performance in ancillary media.

For a mainstream film, calculating the likely box office is usually done on the basis of the performance of similar films in the past. This in turn will allow the distributor to calculate the marketing spend which will be appropriate to the particular kind of film. To predict the likely performance at the box office, the distributor will examine the track record of previous films of a similar genre. But such comparisons always have to be treated with caution, given the singular nature of every film and its dependence on such factors as the effectiveness of its advertising campaign and the word of mouth.

Some distributors, when calculating the appropriate P&A budget for a film, include the amount of potential revenue that can be anticipated from video and television distribution, as well as the expected theatrical gross calculations. The revenues that are expected to be generated by video and television can be set against the P&A budget in this way because the theatrical marketing campaign will serve as a showcase for the film, so that most consumers should already have awareness of the title when it is released in ancillary media. The value of the theatrical marketing campaign is therefore not restricted simply to cinema exhibition alone, but may have a considerable effect on video sales and the value of the film for television.

P&A COSTS IN EUROPE

P&A costs vary widely from country to country depending on the size of the market, and on the possibilities of recouping from theatrical, TV or video release. In the last 10 years, however, the release costs of films have spiralled.

In Europe, although there are no accurate figures available to document the trend, it is widely accepted that P&A costs have risen sharply – tripled over the last seven years, according to some industry experts – primarily as a result of the rising costs of advertising. In the US, the rise in P&A costs has been even more dramatic and, on average, the studios spend almost half of the film's budget on P&A.[26]

---

26 But the members of the Motion Picture Association of America (MPAA), which includes all the Hollywood majors, have tried increasingly hard to contain the explosion in marketing costs. According to MPAA figures, in 1992 the average negative cost of a film produced by an MPAA member company was $28.2 million and the average P&A cost was $13.5 million. In 1991 the average negative cost was $26.1 million and the average P&A cost was $12.1 million.

With P&A costs soaring, cinema admissions falling in many territories, and total revenues concentrated on a smaller number of films – primarily Hollywood titles – the risks for the independent distributor in Europe have increased considerably.

For commercial reasons, the precise marketing costs for specific films tend to be a closely guarded secret and distributors are reluctant to divulge exact P&A expenditure. The practice of discounting rate card prices for advertising media, which is particularly prevalent in countries such as France and Spain, and volume discounts, obtained from servicing companies in return for guaranteeing them a certain level of work, makes the calculation of costs in these territories particularly difficult.

Obtaining reliable P&A costs is further complicated by the fact that although some costs, such as those of prints, tend to be fixed within a narrow band (typically $1095-1460/ECU982-1310), the price of other items, such as dubbing, can vary enormously from country to country.[27]

Even when it is possible to obtain figures on the costs of P&A, these may not include hidden discounts on advertisement space or rebates from film laboratories. This is one of the reasons that sales agents often insist on receiving a minimum guarantee from a distributor, since this assures them that they should receive some money back from the film's distribution rather than seeing all the revenues absorbed by an artificially inflated P&A budget.

However, it is possible to put together some rules of thumb for different types of release in various countries, as an approximate guide to potential marketing budgets.

France

In France, industry estimates are that, for mainstream pictures, the P&A costs range between Fr5-8 million (ECU0.74-1.18 million/$0.82-1.31). For example, the epic 1492 Christopher Columbus, cost Fr77.2 million to produce and had a P&A budget of Fr8 million for a release of 230 prints. On an arthouse film, the P&A costs are likely to range from Fr200,000-1 million. The P&A budget for Man Bites Dog, the Belgian independent film, released by AAA with 28 prints, was Fr800,000.

Sweden

Bertil Sandgren, managing director of Sandrews, a Swedish independent distribution company, estimates the P&A budget for a major 80-print release in that territory would be approximately

---

27 See Dubbing and Subtitling Costs.

$500,000 (ECU448,630). At the other end of the scale, he estimates that a 10-print arthouse release would be budgeted at $150,000.

Switzerland

In Switzerland, Monopole Pathé, which distributed The Commitments, directed by Alan Parker, put up a P&A budget of SFr140,000 (ECU83,360/$92,905) to support an 11-print release.

The UK

In the UK, a reasonable minimum spend would be around £50,000 (ECU65,500/$73,000) on an 8-10 print release, although you can spend just £25,000 on a platform release with little advertising.

DUBBING AND SUBTITLING COSTS

All films released by a distributor which were not shot in a language native to the specific territory will need to be dubbed or subtitled. The cost of this will form part of the P&A budget. While a good dub or excellent subtitling will not be sufficient to rescue a poor film, poor dubbing or indifferent subtitling can certainly hamper the performance of any film. Too often distributors allocate insufficient money for this purpose and sales agents or producers deliver inferior materials, such as poor-quality magnetic soundtracks. This can delay the eventual release of the film, lead to increased costs and adversely effect its box-office potential.

> **The price of dubbing varies considerably according to the length and amount of dialogue in each film, but there is also a wide variation in prices across Europe.**

In some European territories the practice of dubbing prevails, while in others subtitling is preferred (see chart p.124). In Europe, films are most often dubbed in Italy, France, Spain and Germany, for both cultural and economic reasons. However, in France, Spain and Germany subtitled versions of films are generally used in arthouse cinemas in the key cities. A subtitled print is referred to as an Original Version in newspaper listings. In the UK there is no market for dubbed films, and subtitling of foreign films is the norm.

In the smaller territories, such as the Benelux countries, Greece and Portugal, the costs of dubbing are prohibitive, so that subtitling is the norm. In such countries the dominance of English-language films is even greater than in countries where dubbing prevails.

The price of dubbing varies considerably according to the length and amount of dialogue in each film, but there is also a wide variation in prices across Europe. For example, it is particularly expensive in Italy, as a result of demands by the unions representing actors. Figures supplied by UIP and 20th Century Fox indicate the following average costs: Italy ($55,000/ECU48,630), Germany ($48,000), France ($42,000) and Spain ($30,000). However, such costs are amortised across ancillary media as well as on the theatrical release.

Dubbing or subtitling? – The preference within the EC countries

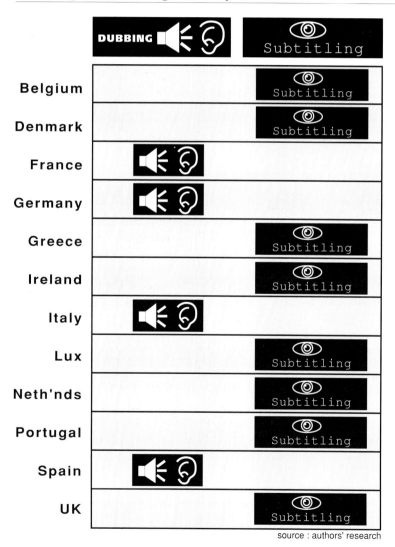

As shown left, the key dubbing countries are four of the largest European markets. Subtitling is preferred in most other territories. However, subtitled prints are sometimes used for arthouse films in France and Spain.

source : authors' research

It takes four to six weeks for a distributor to prepare a foreign version. Ideally, the foreign distributor will need some quality sub-titled or dubbed prints to use in media screenings four to six months in advance of the release of the film. If the critics are obliged to base their review on a poorly dubbed or subtitled version of a film this may adversely affect their opinion of the picture.

For all these reasons it is important that the distributor secures a print as early as possible from the sales agent or producer. The earlier the materials are available to the subtitling or dubbing laboratory, the better the chances of quality results.

SUPPORT SYSTEMS IN EUROPE

Several support schemes, organised on a European and national level, have been created to assist the independent distribution sector in the wake of the high P&A costs which prevail across Europe. The most important pan-European initiative is the European Film Distribution Office (EFDO). There are also a number of national initiatives, of which the two cited below – for Denmark and France – are representative examples.

EUROPEAN FILM DISTRIBUTION OFFICE

The European Film Distribution Office is a pan-European distribution support scheme launched by the Commission of the European Community's MEDIA Programme in 1988. It awards loans to distributors of up to 50% of the costs of launching a film.

> "The most important pan-European initiative is the European Film Distribution Office (EFDO)."

For a picture to qualify for aid, at least three different distributors from three different EC countries or the European Free Trade Area (EFTA) member countries must have agreed to release the film theatrically. The distributors receive up to ECU100,000 ($111,450) towards the release of the film in each territory.

The loan is an advance on receipts which must be reimbursed when the films show a profit, and only films with production costs of up to ECU4.5 million ($5 million) are eligible for the loan. EFDO ultimately expects to be fully reimbursed by all distributors receiving loans, although so far it has only been repaid 20% of its contributions.

EFDO's mandate is threefold: to reduce the distributors' release costs, to permit increased promotion of European films and to increase the level of dialogue and co-operation between European distributors.

Since its inception the distribution programme, based in Hamburg, has supported about 150 films including The Crying Game, Fiorile, and Jamón Jamón, with grants totalling $30 million (ECU27 million). Some 25% of all European distributors have received support from EFDO, on at least one occasion.

FRENCH DISTRIBUTION SUBSIDIES

The Centre National de la Cinématographie (CNC), the French state body that supports the country's film and television industries, offers four different types of subsidy to film distributors:

- Automatic subsidies, given to distributors of French films who reinvest these sums in the production of new films.

- Selective subsidies, given to distributors who exhibit arthouse films which may require particularly careful handling and may present some financial risk.

Within the Selective category, there are two types of subsidy:

- Film subsidy, paying a maximum of Fr500,000 (ECU74,430 /$82,950) towards P&A or print costs (for a maximum of 10 prints) which is reimbursable after a year if the film goes into profit.

- Distribution company subsidy, which ranges from Fr100,000 to Fr1 million (ECU14,800–148,000/$16,490–164,900) per year, although awards between Fr700,000–800,000 (ECU100,000–118,000/$111,450–131,511) are typical.

These state subsidies are allocated to around 15 distribution companies annually. "The goal is to stimulate the advertising and promotion campaigns and diminish the risks taken by the distributors," says Jean-René Marchand, head of the CNC's distribution and exhibition division.

DANISH DISTRIBUTION SUBSIDIES

The Danish Film Institute has a subsidy system which contributes up to half the print costs, based on a special rate negotiated with a local film laboratory. As many as 75 prints can be co-financed by the Danish Film Institute in this way. The idea is to give the distributor the widest number of prints possible with which to open the film, which is particularly important since the opening weeks of the film are the most critical in terms of revenues.

Another support system makes awards for marketing (around $50,000/ECU44,860). The subsidy is a loan which must be repaid before the producer recoups a share of the revenues. Under the terms of this system, a jury from the Danish Film Institute will offer five extra prints of a film as a grant if it shows commercial potential on release. This allows the film to be shown in the provinces sooner, as well as raising the awareness of the title.

Independent distribution in Europe is a high-risk business, as the increased share of the box office claimed by the US majors and the rise in P&A costs put an increasing squeeze on distributors.

The limited P&A resources available to European independent distributors has had the effect of making Europeans work particularly hard to maximise creativity and cost-effectiveness.

Once the P&A budget has been set, the distributor must determine the most effective way to spend the money, with the goal of attracting the largest possible audience to see the picture.

THE ESSENTIAL INGREDIENTS OF AN ADVERTISING CAMPAIGN

As well as deciding on the best release date for a film and making sure that it is available to as many targeted cinemas as possible, the distributor's skill lies in increasing awareness of the film as well as the specific desire of the audience to see the film – the want to see factor. The usual means to achieve these goals are through advertising, publicity and promotion.

In a business where the first few days are critical in determining commercial success or failure, the distributor's decision on how to position a film – together with the level of spending on advertising and publicity and the way in which that money is targeted – will have a crucial impact on the film's life. The failure to market a picture effectively may seriously limit its potential audience, even in the case of those films, which on paper at least, appear to have all the ingredients of a box-office hit.

The marketing for European pictures often lacks the financial power of US blockbusters. As a result there is a sharp divide between most mainstream US films which are heavily marketed and have a high awareness level, such as Jurassic Park, and many European films which do not have the same resources. However, as Jean Labadie, chief executive officer of French independent distribution company Bac Films, argues, this is where creativity, ingenuity and an intimate knowledge of the local market can benefit European distributors, enabling them to overcome the disadvantages of a limited budget.

For mainstream films, advance advertising often creates the highest levels of awareness, interest and want to see. Specialist films will rely less on advertising prior to their release, but more effort will be concentrated on the release and post-release periods to encourage word of mouth, and to try to convince the exhibitors to keep playing the films.

Because limited P&A budgets may restrict their ability to the breadth of their paid advertising campaigns, European distributors often undertake comprehensive publicity and promotion campaigns. These are designed to promote editorial coverage, especially reviews as well as word of mouth, and can be highly effective marketing tools. The most effective campaigns will combine paid advertising with a well-planned and executed publicity campaign.

The following section will examine the creation and use of marketing materials, starting with materials used in paid advertising. It will then move on to consider the role of publicity and promotion in the distribution campaign.

THE ADVERTISING CAMPAIGN

OVERALL PLANNING

For European films which do not have a distribution deal in their home country before they commence production, the producer and the director or the international sales agent usually supervise the use of creative materials (such as the poster and trailer) in the marketing campaign. These can subsequently be adapted for each national market.

Given that the goal is to market the picture to the general public, the distributor may have a strategic advantage as compared with the producer or director when it comes to designing the marketing tools. The director (and producer) will be primarily concerned with realising their vision of the film, and may simply be too close to the project to be able to conceive the most effective way of attracting the general public, although their input into this process can still be extremely useful.

The distributor with a knowledge of the marketplace is arguably better positioned than the producer or director to create tools such as the poster and trailer which will be effective in attracting the target audience.

If a distribution deal is already in place for a film before production starts, the marketing department of the distributor will usually develop the marketing tools together with the producer and the director. In this instance, the materials will often be adapted to the needs of the market from the inception of the project.

> **" The distributor with a knowledge of the marketplace is arguably better positioned than the producer or director to create marketing tools. "**

The distributor subsequently hires creative agencies (to design the poster and make the trailer) and advertising agencies (to book the advertising space); they will usually come back with ideas based on the distributor's marketing brief. These agencies often work closely with either the in-house public relations agent of the distributor or a public relations agency hired to help market the film. But since they are paying the bills, it is the distributor who will maintain final control of the campaign.

Most European distributors stress that producers should always include the costs of basic marketing materials in their initial production budget. This will save time and money, as well as improving the quality of the promotional material produced. Without a unit publicist and photographer working on marketing material during production, the distributor will have to invest far more in P&A for the film at the release stage, since it will then be more expensive to secure special shots of the cast or director.

PHOTOGRAPHS

For the European distributor, photographs will form a crucial part of the advertising campaign. They are vital in creating a visual image for the film since few distributors will be able to afford television advertising, and photographs can be used in posters and for distributing to the press.[28] Before the start of principal photography, the producer and distributor should ensure that they will be able to secure high-quality black-and-white and colour photographs while the film is shooting.

---

28 In any case, in France, television advertising of films is not permitted.

It will be considerably more difficult (and costly) to try to shoot photographs after principal photography has finished. For example, the cast may have moved on to other films, and it may be impossible to secure photographs featuring more than one individual. Moreover, photographs taken on set will be much more effective in conveying the tone of the film.

For example, European directors such as Bernardo Bertolucci and Pedro Almodovar are very aware of the importance of stills as a means of securing publicity for a film. In the build-up to the release of their pictures they will ensure that high-quality stills are widely available to the press, and this combined with a high-profile public relations campaign ensures that their films attract considerable press attention.

Wherever possible, the distributor should aim to hire a professional unit photographer who will shoot from a brief given by the producer, distributor or unit publicist. As colour can be converted to black-and-white, it is usually advisable to shoot 60% of the photographs in colour and 40% in black-and-white. Apart from guaranteeing stills coverage – which can be used to sell the film to the industry, the press, the exhibitors and the general audience – these photographs can also be incorporated in the artwork for the film's poster.

In some countries, such as France, it is common practice for producers to hire photo agencies, such as Sygma or Gamma, as the number of professional unit photographers has greatly diminished. The agency pays the photographer, gives some photographs to the producer and/or distributor and keeps the others to sell to magazines around the world. However, this does not always help in the marketing of a film. The agency might keep the rights to the photographs, so depriving the producer and/or distributor of their licence to use the visuals as they would wish.

> " Too often, European producers and distributors overlook the importance of photographs. "

US production companies tend to be much more effective at supplying quality photographic material, well in advance of the eventual release, making it easier for distributors to prepare their campaign. Too often European producers and distributors overlook the importance of photographs.

CREATING THE POSTER AND ARTWORK

In Europe, where the qualitative aspect of a marketing campaign is more important than the quantitative, the poster is the primary medium for advertising the film. As the poster focuses the attention of a wide audience on a specific film, the message it is likely to convey to the audience about the film needs to be studied carefully. The process of creating the poster for the public distribution of the film is broadly similar to that described for international pre-sales, as outlined above in Section Four: Markets and Festivals.

The percentage of the marketing budget spent on producing the poster is relatively low in terms of the total P&A. It is the buying of the space for the posters which will constitute a more significant item of the budget. But as the poster will also form the basis of the advertisements which will be placed in the press, its importance cannot be under-estimated and distributors must ensure that they invest wisely to secure the most effective image for their film.

In the first stage of the development of the poster, the distributor and in-house creative personnel meet with the advertising agencies and the various designers that have been retained to create the visuals for the picture.

All those involved are shown a rough cut of the film or the completed film if the print is available. If no footage is ready, the designers work with the script and any photographs that are available from the shoot. The distributor will often have a specific conception on how to position the film to its audience, and will work closely with the designer to ensure that this conception is realised.

In Europe, some producers and distributors are not afraid of hiring a pool of designers to develop as many as 30-40 different visual images, so as to find a campaign which has the best possible chance of maximising the audience for the film.

As a result of cost constraints, some European distributors choose to adapt the original poster campaign, created in the country where the film originated, to their local market. If they are generally satisfied with the material provided by the producer or sales agent, they may simply make slight modifications, for instance by adding taglines in the local language. In some cases, the same basic poster may be used across many different territories.

But different poster formats used in various European territories can still create additional printing costs for the distributor (see chart p.132).

By contrast, in the case of US films, particularly the kind of mainstream pictures handled by the US majors, the same campaign will often be used across most territories in which the film is released. This is largely a testament to the power of the Hollywood marketing machine whose norms and values are familiar to audiences throughout the world.

Poster dimensions in 6 EC countries (figures in mm)

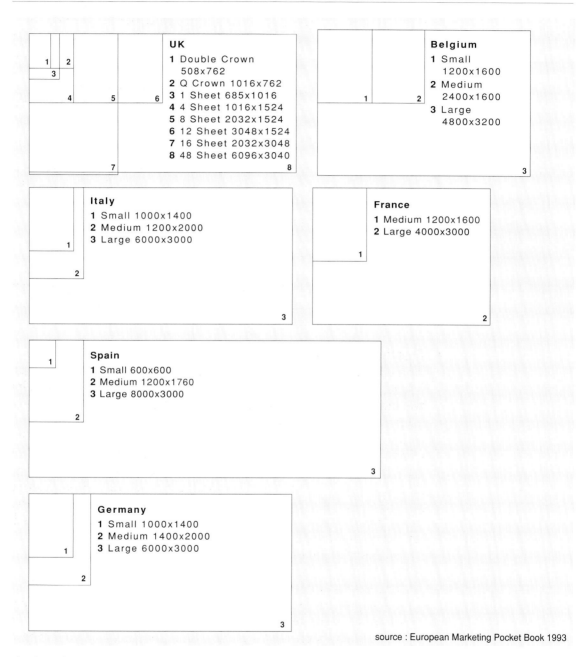

UK
1 Double Crown
   508x762
2 Q Crown 1016x762
3 1 Sheet 685x1016
4 4 Sheet 1016x1524
5 8 Sheet 2032x1524
6 12 Sheet 3048x1524
7 16 Sheet 2032x3048
8 48 Sheet 6096x3040

Belgium
1 Small
   1200x1600
2 Medium
   2400x1600
3 Large
   4800x3200

Italy
1 Small 1000x1400
2 Medium 1200x2000
3 Large 6000x3000

France
1 Medium 1200x1600
2 Large 4000x3000

Spain
1 Small 600x600
2 Medium 1200x1760
3 Large 8000x3000

Germany
1 Small 1000x1400
2 Medium 1400x2000
3 Large 6000x3000

source : European Marketing Pocket Book 1993

The chart above shows how the sizes of posters vary across the different EC countries. For example, the small size of posters in Belgium corresponds to a medium size in other countries while the large size in Spain is twice as broad as the large size in France.

London is an important centre for the production of marketing materials, since that is where many of the largest international sales companies are based.[29] According to Martin Butterworth of The Creative Partnership, one of the leading poster companies in London, producing the poster will cost on average £5000 (ECU6550/$7300) – £1000 for the printing in two formats, £2000 for the design and £2000 for the computer-generated image.

Paris is another important centre for poster making. It is the biggest film capital in Europe and the prohibition of television advertising for films has underlined the importance of the poster as an advertising medium. In France the total cost of producing a poster is slightly higher than in the UK and is generally reckoned to be between Fr60,000-150,000 (ECU8900-22,250/$9919-24,797).

The importance of these two centres – London and Paris – is reflected in the fact that the English or French poster campaigns are often re-used throughout Europe.

The poster artwork can include illustrations, photographs and graphics. If there are no photographs to work with, designers can still combine images in a montage using computer graphics, although this will add to the cost.

- ## Creating the Copy for the Poster

  The copy is the text on the poster that, in emphasising the visual image, plays a vital role in selling the film to the audience. It helps the cinema goer to relate to the film by highlighting the names of stars or the director or other relevant ingredients.

  In some European territories, the poster copy will also often consist of taglines, emphasising a particular aspect of the story, certain awards that the film has won, or the track record of the director and stars. Posters advertising US films throughout Europe will also include taglines. The use of taglines tends to be more prevalent in northern Europe. Some countries such as France will not use them for indigenous films.

  Taglines will usually highlight the following:

  - **The dramatic elements of the story.** These might include love, danger, adventure, mystery etc. The UK poster for Damage featured a tagline with just two words: "Desire, Deceit". For the UK campaign on High Heels, the tagline read: "What happens when a daughter marries her mother's lover?"

---

29 See Section Three: International Sales.

- **The awards**. On posters for films that have won a prize in Cannes, Venice or Berlin, the logo of the particular award may be featured, or the text may mention prizes won by the director or the cast.

- **The stars or director**. Previous films from particular director, or featuring specific stars will be mentioned if they have achieved box-office success. For example, in the UK, Jim Jarmusch's Night on Earth was promoted as the new film "from the director of Down By Law and Mystery Train" and Stephen Frears' The Snapper, from the book by Roddy Doyle, was billed as the film from "the director of Dangerous Liaisons and the writer of The Commitments".

In some European countries the poster copy may also feature quotes from critics, praising particular aspects of the film or its overall entertainment value. It is not just the nature of the quote but also its source which will be important in determining its effectiveness. For instance, with a mainstream commercial film, a distributor will usually try to use quotes from mass-circulation newspapers since this will constitute a stamp of approval for the target audience of the film. For arthouse films, a positive review from critics of quality newspapers or magazines can have a decisive impact on the potential cinema goer.

The visuals with these quotes are then placed in key newspapers and magazines to target the appropriate audience, or used as display or one-sheet advertisements in cinema lobbies.

As the audience may be judging the merits of one film against another on the basis of the poster, it is arguable that the absence of taglines or copy quotes on posters for films in certain countries may hurt the effectiveness of the marketing campaign.

The billing on a poster lists the talent (producer, director, stars) and crew that contributed to the film's production. Designers are often under contractual obligation as to the positioning and size of the names on any promotional material. The larger the film, the more specific will be such obligations. For instance, certain names of the cast on the poster may have to be 25% of the size of the artwork of the title as well as being in a certain position.

- ### Positioning the Poster

Most posters are used at outdoor sites, although some will also be put up in the cinemas themselves. Expenditure on outdoor posters in Europe is relatively high – in France, for example, posters may account for as much as two-thirds of the total advertising budget while in the US expenditure on outdoor posters often represents less than 1%. The poster campaign will generally start two weeks before the release of the film and continue during the week of the release. To maximise the effect of poster advertising, distributors often complement the campaign with **flyposting** in which posters are unofficially put up on walls and buildings.

Although outdoor posters can be placed in specific geographical areas, the targeting of the audience remains relatively inexact since such billboards mainly reach mass urban audiences that are difficult to place in sub-groups. In the major European cities, positions for outdoor posters include underground trains, buses, bus shelters and roadside billboards.

However, outdoor posters can be highly cost-effective. They usually reach the core audience of cinema goers (urban, 15-35) who use public transport every day. They can also be used at strategic sites close to cinemas. Furthermore, by using the same visual on posters, advertisements and in foyers of cinemas, a high level of awareness can be achieved.

In each country, poster spaces will be booked from a national or local sales house, or through an advertising agency. In some countries, such as France, there is a relatively limited amount of poster space available because of the high level of competition between distributors. This means that such bookings have to be made anywhere from 4 to 12 months in advance. This can create problems for independent distribution companies that have little power over the release date of their films. Although it is still possible to strike deals at the last minute, this may not always allow sufficient time for the poster to be printed.

The high degree of competition for outdoor sites in France has led the sales houses to offer new types of site. For example, Metrobus, the advertising sales house for the public transport company RATP, is selling spaces on handrails and entry doors in the underground railway system. These are ideal locations as they are relatively inexpensive and there is a high volume of pedestrian traffic in such areas.

In the cinemas, the posters will be highly visible. The advantage of positioning them in cinemas is that the poster will always reach the cinema goer.

For a major release, a teaser poster is often created to precede the appearance of the main poster. The teaser poster usually presents just a few details of the film, which are designed to incite the interest of the audience so that they will seek more information about the film. If a teaser poster campaign is used it usually starts to appear four to five weeks before release.

CENSORSHIP

In each European territory, local authorities or national film censorship boards may have statutory rights to review marketing material to determine whether it is deemed likely to cause public offence. When the distributor is creating the marketing campaign it is important to bear in mind the possibility of censorship.

For example in the UK, where censorship is particularly strict, posters showing guns pointing at people or men looming over women are prohibited. The London Transport Authority, which operates the city's buses and underground railways, will expect to see the artwork for any film with an 18 certificate, if posters are to be put up on its billboards.

CREATING AND USING THE TRAILER

The trailer for a film can be one of the most effective marketing tools as it directly addresses the cinema goer. It is usually the first sales tool to appear, preceding the poster and other forms of advertising. Unlike other forms of advertising, the trailer allows the audience to sample the film directly, a fact which enhances its importance. As a consequence, the trailer can play a crucial factor in determining audience response to the film (see Section Six). Ideally, the trailer should first play in the cinema around six weeks before the release of the film, and keep playing until the picture opens in the cinema.

> " Unlike other forms of advertising, the trailer allows the audience to sample the film directly. "

A trailer has four main functions:

- To create awareness of the title.

- To impart an overall impression of the film to its potential audience.

- To ensure that the audience is aware of the film's director and of the main stars, in cases where such names will help sell the picture.

- To create want to see among the potential audience.

Trailers are made by specialist companies or – as is often the case for European films with small or medium budgets – by the director or the film editor.

The trailer company will usually work in consultation with the film's producer, director, distributor – and, where relevant, the sales agent – seeking to identify those marketable elements of the film which will make the most effective trailer. Unlike posters, there are no contractual obligations with a trailer although, in certain cases, the director may have the right of approval over the trailer.[30]

Trailers for certain types of film, such as those with cross-over potential, will have to attempt to create appeal for different segments of the audience. For example, the campaign for certain male-oriented films may need to be constructed in such a way that the picture has some appeal to (or at least does not completely repel) females who might accompany the target male audience to the cinema.

The trailer is usually cut from the release print of the film and will require both a script and music. The ideal length for a trailer is between 90-120 seconds. If it is any longer the exhibitor may be reluctant to play it. On bigger releases, the distributor usually makes three or four trailers for every print of a film.

The distributor should allow between six to eight weeks to complete the trailer. The average budget for a trailer on a European film (excluding the cost of printing in laboratories) is £10,000 (ECU13,100/$14,600)

When European distributors are handling US films they will usually adapt the existing trailer campaign in some way. Re-editing will be used to tone down the trailer since US trailers often tend to use a hard-sell approach, with fast cuts and repetition of key scenes from the film. The US trailer may also be re-voiced and its length adjusted. To be able to adapt an existing trailer makes things much cheaper, with such a process costing between £2000-4000 (ECU2620-5240/$2920-5840).

TEASER TRAILERS

Teaser trailers use a combination of footage from the film, still photography and graphics, and are designed to give a very brief glimpse of the film with the goal of arousing the audience's curiosity. The ideal length for a teaser trailer is around 30 seconds, as this gives it a strong chance of being inserted in the exhibitor's trailer reel.

Teasers will usually only be used on mainstream films which will have a wide release backed by a high P&A budget. The teaser

---

30 For example, this usually applies to films originated in France, where the droit moral gives the director final cut on material.

trailer should ideally play two to three months before the film's release. For blockbuster films from the US majors, the teaser trailer might play as much as six months in advance of release. The cost of creating a teaser trailer and trailer can be as much as £15,000 (ECU19,650/$21,900).

- **Getting the Trailer Played**
  Even a first-class trailer is useless if it does not play regularly in the cinema. Differences in the perceived value of trailers are a constant source of tension between distributors and exhibitors. Many distributors feel that exhibitors often do not give sufficient emphasis to trailers. It is the distributor's responsibility to ensure that trailers are being played as there will be no formal contract with the exhibitor.

  Exhibitors will usually play trailers in batches of three or four after the advertisements for a film. They will often sacrifice playing more trailers in favour of increasing the time for screen advertising. Their argument is that they do not directly benefit from trailers, unlike screen advertising which comprises an important source of revenue. To compensate for not playing trailers on screen, some exhibitors are now playing them on video monitors in their cinema foyers.

> **" Even a first-class trailer is useless if it does not play regularly in the cinema. "**

  If a distributor cannot get the trailer to play it may be necessary to buy screen advertising time from one of the companies responsible for selling such time. Although this may be expensive, it guarantees that the film is shown to the targeted audience. The booking company will target the trailer for showing in certain geographical zones (national, regional or local cinemas), in particular types of cinema or with specific films.

  The positioning of the trailer in the right cinema at the right time is as important as the positioning of the print itself. Trailers are usually played alongside films of a style or genre similar to that of the film being trailed. If it is felt that a film has cross-over potential, on the other hand, there may be some advantage in screening the trailer before a film of a rather different type, in an attempt to broaden the audience.

  Certain exhibition companies which are owned by groups with interests in distribution may give preference to trailers which advertise films being handled by the distributors to which they are tied. This can make it harder for independent distributors to place their trailers in such cinemas.

As with so many aspects of the marketing process, timing is crucial. A very effective trailer that is delivered late or not at all is useless. Equally, a distributor may need to exercise negotiating muscle with reluctant exhibitors to ensure that their trailers are played.

CREATING AND USING PRESS ADVERTISING

In Europe, press advertising is important for informing the audience as to when and where the film will play. After the film's release, newspaper advertising can reinforce the level of awareness and the want to see factor. The primary medium for press advertising is newspapers, although film and entertainment magazines and other publications may be used, depending on the target audience.

The print media advertising campaign usually starts two weeks prior to the opening of the film. The press campaign will usually draw on the poster for its visual images, but may also include quotes from selected reviews in some territories, especially in northern Europe. A proportion of the press advertising spend should be budgeted to support the film after its initial opening, to help sustain word of mouth.

Teaser advertising campaigns, which use just a few details of the film, may start anywhere from three to four weeks before the opening of the picture. Such teaser campaigns can be an effective way of highlighting audience expectation.

Press advertising has the advantage of short lead times, since for daily and weekly publications, advertisements can usually be booked just a few days in advance. The impact of such advertising is short-lived, however, especially in the case of daily publications. Over the past 10 years, the use of print media advertisements in Europe has gradually declined, in part as a result of the growth of television advertising. In France, the use of posters has overtaken the print media (see chart p.140).

The decline in expenditure on print advertising can also be ascribed to the changing nature of the relationship between distributors and the print media in recent years. Increasingly, distributors are striking promotional deals with the press, giving away cinema seats in return for free advertising space.

Distributors may also use *advertorial*, which combines advertising with editorial, to increase awareness of the film. For example, during the French campaign for Man Bites Dog, advertising agency Tennessee placed a four-page insertion in the French magazine Actuel, in the monthly issue prior to the film's release. The supplement was written in the same satirical spirit as the maga-

Share of film advertising spend by media in the UK and France

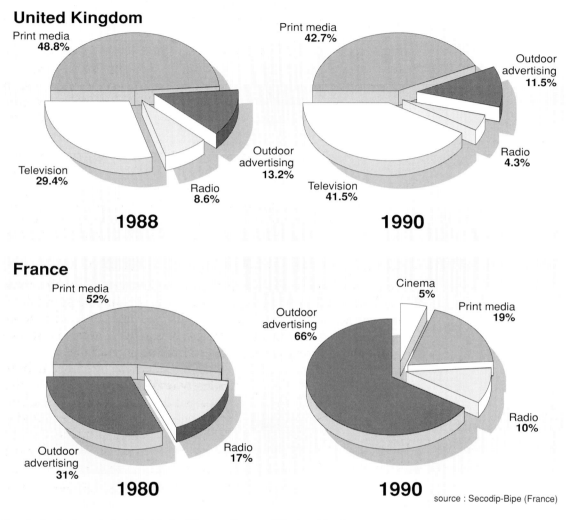

The pie charts above indicate that in the UK expenditure on TV advertising has increased dramatically within just two years. Because of a ban on TV advertising of films in France, outdoor advertising is the leading medium, having superseded print media, which was the favoured outlet during the early 1980s.

zine. In order to reach the target audience, Tennessee's marketing consultant Monique Bondil, the advertising co-ordinator, distributed prints of the advertorial in universities and colleges in Paris. The result was a substantial increase in awareness and want to see among the target audience.

CREATING AND USING TELEVISION ADVERTISING

The same companies that make trailers often also specialise in creating television campaigns for a feature film. Because of the cost of airtime, it is usually only high-budget films which can afford a television campaign.

The length of a television spot is usually between 10-30 seconds. It is often a shorter version of the trailer and follows the same production procedure: scripting, selecting and editing. Creating such spots can cost anything from £2000 (ECU2620/$2920) up to a maximum of £15,000 for a large campaign. The voice-over can be particularly expensive.

Television campaigns are usually timed to start 5 to 10 days before a film opens, and if a picture is performing strongly, it may be continued during the first week of release.

Television advertising for films is used heavily in the US. The various different forms of television, such as network, cable and syndication, offer numerous opportunities to reach specific targeted audiences.

In Europe, television advertising is used much less, primarily because the high costs mean that it is beyond the reach of the P&A budget for most films. In many cases, the high cost of television airtime means that European distributors may find it more cost-effective to invest in electronic press kits that can be shown free of charge during news or entertainment programmes.

In France, television advertising of theatrical movies has been banned since 1969. The film industry originally supported the ban since it was partly aimed at curbing the power of the broadcasters, and of the major theatrical distributors who are the only groups who could afford it. Negotiations to lift the ban are underway, as it is seen as an impediment to many marketing campaigns.

> **In France, television advertising of theatrical movies has been banned since 1969.**

Television advertising for films is most common in Germany, Italy and the UK. In Italy, if the state broadcaster RAI has co-produced a film, or bought the television rights to it, it will usually offer discount advertising time for the picture.

Satellite television is also increasingly being used in Europe as an advertising medium for mainstream releases. Many satellite channels are aimed at specific segments of the population, and offer distributors the chance to reach targeted audiences. MTV Europe, in particular, is used to reach cinema goers in the 16-24 age bracket – UIP used the channel heavily in the marketing campaign for Wayne's World.

CREATING AND USING RADIO ADVERTISING

The radio campaign will often be created by the same company that created the trailer for a film. For radio, the ideal advertising slot is about 30 seconds, although shorter spots of 10-15 seconds may also be produced. Radio advertising is usually used to increase levels of awareness and interest in the run-up to the opening of the film and during the first weeks of release. The first spots will usually air two to three days in advance of release. Radio is often used simultaneously with television ads for large campaigns, and as a means to reinforce the good reviews if the film has opened well.

For the Spanish release of The Hairdresser's Husband, the distributor Surf Films used radio spots featuring favourable *vox pops* as a means of enticing more cinema goers in the wake of the initial release.

For campaigns with a more restricted budget, radio spots offer an attractive alternative to television spots as they are cheaper. Radio is also an ideal medium for targeting particular groups, since many stations are aimed at specific segments of the population. For this reason, it is vital to choose the right slot on the right station in order to reach the targeted audience.

Radio will be extremely valuable in the case of films which have a strong soundtrack, such as Strictly Ballroom or Tous les Matins du Monde. It can also be particularly effective for youth-oriented films, since this group tends to spend a relatively large amount of time listening to radio. For specialised films, radio spots are often too expensive, but distributors of such films have increasing access to discounts as part of promotional deals with radio stations.

MARKET RESEARCH

WHAT IS MARKET RESEARCH? One method of testing the likely impact of a particular marketing strategy is market research. This can help assess whether a film has been positioned in a way that is likely to appeal to its potential audience.

Market research is rarely used in Europe, unlike in the US, where it is perceived as a quasi-scientific tool and used to gain a comprehensive knowledge of the state of the marketplace as well as to test the appeal of elements of the film ranging from story content to the nature of the marketing campaign. It is thus very useful for assessing the potential effectiveness of posters or trailers

"" If few European independent distributors use market research, it is largely because of cost. ""

prior to release, and it helps the distributor to determine the most effective means of positioning a film.

If few European independent distributors use market research, it is largely because of cost. In the UK, the average cost of a playability study is £6000 (ECU7860/$8760) per film. Indeed, market research costs are so high that even the studios, with their considerable financial muscle, pool their resources to cover the costs of such research.[31]

In Europe, there is also a widespread cultural resistance to market research, since in many cases films are perceived as personal and intimate works of art, rather than as product that can be re-shaped to fit the demands of the marketplace.

In the US, a variety of research tools have been developed to assist in the marketing and distribution of films.[32] The goal of such research is to construct the most successful marketing strategy possible for each release. The research findings are used to assess the following factors, some of which have been discussed in a different context earlier in this section:

PLAYABILITY

How do audiences respond to the film after having seen it? Do they like it? Will they recommend it to friends? Which types of film goer, based on demographic and lifestyle attributes, rate it best? Are these groups large enough to open the picture and will their word of mouth be credible?

POSITIONING

Which, of all the possible ways of selling the film, including combining different major and minor storylines, characters, and personnel (including actors, directors, screenwriters and producers) gives the film appeal to the widest audience? Does the target audience coincide with the types of film goer which rate the picture the highest? Is there a discrepancy between the playability and the marketability of the film, and how can this be resolved?

---

31 At the Media Business School Master Class in Film Marketing held in Antwerp, June 30th-July 2nd 1992, Duncan Clark suggested that the European film industry might co-opt interested parties such as soft-drinks manufacturers to help finance such research, since they had the same target audience.

---

32 This section was developed from material kindly supplied by Dr. Joseph Helfgot, president of Marketcast, a US-based company specialising in market research for the film industry.

MARKETING MATERIALS

What specific marketing materials (posters, trailers, print ads, promotional campaigns) need to be developed in order creatively to reflect the most successful positioning strategy for the film? Do these stimulate the desire to see the film?

RELEASE DATE

What release date will work best for a specific film, given the competition from other films that will open at around the same time (this includes a window of two weeks before and one week after the selected date)? The goal is to avoid competition which will steal a proportion of your core audience.

MEDIA AND ADVERTISING

Given the target markets for the film's playability and marketability, which media are most appropriate given what is available in each territory where the film is to open? It is also important to identify the other films with which the trailer should be playing so that the target audience is reached in the most effective manner.

There are several specific tools which are used to achieve these goals. Research screenings will enable audience response to be tested thoroughly. The audience at such special screenings, held in advance of the release of the film, will be primarily composed of avids, those film goers who go to the cinema at least once a fortnight, and who will be highly influential in distributing word of mouth on the film. Those invited to attend such screenings will consist of both the target audience for the film and a much wider cross-section of the population.

Positioning analysis will be used to identify those marketing elements of the film that interest people most by evaluating the appeal of each element in relation to all other elements. The goal of the positioning analysis will be to determine the most opportune date for the film's release, to identify which media will be most effective in reaching the target audience for the picture, and to test the appeal of selected marketing hooks before the campaign is created.

There will also be some testing of the creative materials, such as print advertising, posters and trailers, conducted during the market research. This often represents the most costly element of the process, since a large number of revisions tend to be made to the material, with each version of the materials being thoroughly tested. The sheer expense of such work puts it beyond the reach of many of the smaller film distributors.

The research company will also engage in movie tracking, in which the advertising for major film releases is tracked for five weeks before the release of the film and for several weeks after in order to evaluate whether it is hitting its intended target. In effect, this measures awareness of the film. Respondents are also asked whether the advertising has made them desire to see the film, so that it also measures interest in the picture.

HOW IS MARKET RESEARCH USED?

In Europe, the distribution subsidiaries of the majors may use market research once a film opens in a particular market. UIP also uses exit polls in the first two or three markets where the film is released to determine the likely effectiveness of the marketing campaign for the film in other territories. The company analyses the public's reaction during the opening weekend and uses this information to market the film in other territories.

The London-based arm of The National Research Group (NRG), an American company based in London, is often used by the European arms of the US majors.

Despite the high cost of market research, some European independent distributors do undertake research on a more limited basis. They will test-screen films with selected audiences to determine the most effective way in which to position a film. As a result of these screenings, they may change the poster for a film or even alter the title in the local language to suit better the local audience.

For example, in Italy, Life International arranged test screenings of Kafka, directed by Steven Soderbergh. These screenings established that the audience thought they were going to see a film about the life of Kafka, although the film itself was more of a thriller.

As a result, the distributor decided to change the Italian title to Delitti e Segreti (Crimes and Secrets) and positioned the film as a thriller, as it contained a strong element of mystery. He used a poster with the caption "Uno strano scrittore, una donna misteriosa, una serie di oscuri delitti" (A strange writer, a mysterious woman, a series of obscure misdemeanours) to evoke this element of mystery. In doing so, he was able to change the audience's perception of the film.

Other distributors, for example Claude-Eric Poiroux, managing director of Forum Distribution in France, have acknowledged that some past mistakes (for instance, in the construction of the poster

KEY POINTS OF ADVERTISING STRATEGIES

TIME
- For the creation of all the marketing tools, a distributor needs to allow sufficient time – at least two, and preferably three, months.

MATERIALS
- The distributor must get original materials from the film's producer or sales agent so that there is enough time to adapt them for release in a particular country.

PAID ADVERTISING
- Paid advertising usually has the most direct impact on the potential audience.

PHOTOGRAPHS
- Photographs will form a crucial part of the advertising campaign, providing a good basis for creating the film's visual image. Hire a professional unit photographer who will shoot on location – 60% in colour and 40% in black-and-white.

THE POSTER AND ARTWORK
- The poster campaign, the primary medium for advertising the film, will generally start two weeks before the release of the film and continue during the week of the release. In some cases European distributors will adapt the original poster campaign – created by the sales agent or production company in the country where the film originated – to the local market. In other instances, an entirely new poster will be created. As the poster is the primary medium for advertising films in Europe, it is advisable to develop as many images as are needed to get the best image for the film.

THE COPY
- Use catchphrases underlining the key elements of the film, or highlight awards won or names of director or cast in the poster copy. Quotes from approving critics and taglines used on the poster also help to reinforce the image and make the poster more effective.

THE TRAILER

- Ideally, the trailer should first play in the cinema around six weeks before the release of the film, and keep playing until the picture opens in the cinema. Teaser trailers can run anywhere from 6-12 weeks prior to release. If the exhibitor declines to play a trailer, it may be necessary to buy advertising time as a way of getting the trailer screened.

PRESS ADVERTISING

- The primary medium for press advertising is newspapers. The print media advertising campaign usually starts two weeks prior to the opening of the film. Press advertising has the advantage of short lead times, since for daily and weekly publications, advertisements can usually be booked just a few days in advance.

TELEVISION ADVERTISING

- Because of the cost of airtime, it is usually only high-budget films which can afford a television campaign. Television campaigns are usually timed to start 5-10 days before a film opens, and if a picture is performing strongly, it may be continued during the first week of release. Satellite television is increasingly being used in Europe as an advertising medium for large mainstream releases, as it is usually aimed at specific segments of the population.

RADIO ADVERTISING

- Can be a powerful tool for reinforcing the message of the poster and trailer, particularly if the film has a strong soundtrack. Radio advertising, which is considerably cheaper than television, is usually used for mainstream films or titles with cross-over potential, although targeted radio stations – a jazz station or a classical station, for example – might be appropriate for the advertising of specialist films.

MARKET RESEARCH

- Can give the distributor greater control over the marketing materials and advance insight into audience reaction.

campaign) have made them more positively inclined toward market research. As a result, they are prepared to test-screen films to see if the message conveyed by the poster corresponds to the audience's view of the film. "Most independent distributors work on the basis of instinct, but the theatrical market in Europe is too uncertain for instinct alone to be effective," Poiroux says. "Distributors must exercise greater control over the impact of a campaign over the audience."

THE PUBLICITY AND PROMOTIONAL CAMPAIGN

To counterbalance their competitive disadvantage against the US majors, European independent distributors complement advertising with publicity and promotion. The success of European films depends heavily on reviews and word of mouth. Publicity and promotion are marketing tools of equal if not greater importance than advertising. It is important, therefore, to examine how they operate.

The aim of the publicity campaign is to secure editorial coverage of a specific film in media which will be seen by the target audience for a film. It can be a much cheaper method of securing public attention for a film than paid advertising, but the two approaches will usually be used in tandem. Publicity supports the advertising spend. Both publicity and promotion can be enormously helpful in increasing word of mouth on a film.

The publicist or press attaché for a film will seek to arrange interviews between selected media and the film's director and stars. They will also include the widespread circulation of publicity materials to the media. Press screenings of a film will also be arranged for the purpose of securing reviews and for promoting word of mouth so that people will recommend the film to their friends and colleagues.

> " Publicity supports the advertising spend. Both publicity and promotion can be enormously helpful in increasing word of mouth on a film. "

The publicity campaign for a film will often be handled by a publicist working for a public relations company. Several such companies specialise in the film industry. Many European publicists are individuals working on a freelance basis. Some larger distributors may have their own in-house publicist. Some distributors hire different press officers for each film, choosing them according to their taste, their approach to a specific film and their creativity and relations with the press.[33]

The amount of press coverage a film receives will depend on its subject matter (it will help if the story has topical relevance), the cast, the director and, of course, the publicist's contacts in the media and their ability to place stories. With the fierce competition for film coverage in the print and audiovisual media, the publicist has to be creative – especially in the case of specialised films – in finding different angles for different publications and different media.

Promotion is intimately linked to the publicity and advertising activities and is often co-ordinated by the same individuals responsible for marketing. Like the publicity campaign, the ultimate goal of the promotional effort is to increase levels of awareness, want to see and word of mouth. It covers activities ranging from premieres intended to build word of mouth to the licensing and merchandising of characters or objects from the film, which can be used in different ways.

The following two sections examine strategies for maximising the effectiveness of publicity and promotional campaigns.

STRATEGIES FOR MAXIMISING PUBLICITY

CREATING THE STRATEGY

The first task of the publicist is to secure coverage for the film in the entertainment and arts features of the targeted media. The latter will be determined by the way in which the film has been positioned and by the profile of its target audience. To maximise the chances of securing coverage the publicist will try to make the film a newsworthy event. This may help secure coverage in the news or political section of a newspaper, in addition to editorial in the entertainment section. In the case of specialised films, this can help the film cross over from its original audience to a wider public.

Journalists and editors are looking for stories which will sell their publications and it is the task of the publicist to convince them that they have something which will interest the readers of a

---

33 As outlined in Section Three, in some cases publicists are hired by producers or sales agents to supervise the preparation of publicity materials and guarantee media coverage during the pre-production/production stages and during film festivals. The same publicist will invariably handle the campaign for a film once it is completed.

> **Journalists and editors are looking for stories which will sell their publications.**

given publication. As such, in their battle for editorial space, publicists for a particular film may face competition not only from other films but also from a wider range of general interest stories. It is therefore important to start approaching journalists as early as possible in order to secure coverage.

The editorial strategy for obtaining media coverage is constructed by the distributor, the publicist and the promoter. They will consider what type of media coverage is most appropriate for the film, when interviews can best be co-ordinated with the stars and when to show the film to the media. The publicity campaign begins, ideally, three to six months before the opening date.

The publicist is heavily dependent on the quality of the materials provided by the producer, distributor or sales company, with photographs being particularly important.

If stills have not been prepared in advance or their quality is poor, the effectiveness of the publicity campaign can be seriously undermined.

This highlights once again the importance for all concerned of ensuring that unit photographers are attached to films, and that they secure high-quality stills.

In the pre-release period, the publicist will track the available publicity materials, assemble the press kit, organise the press screenings, check the availability of the stars and the director and prepare their schedule of interviews.

THE INGREDIENTS OF THE PRESS KIT

The publicist should ideally commence work on the film at least three to four months before the film's release. The first task is to assemble the press kit for the written media, the electronic press kit (EPK) if the budget allows for one, and the stills.

Press kits usually include cast and list credits, production notes, stills, biographies and filmographies of the cast, director and producer. They should also contain details of the film's release. The electronic press kit will contain many of the same items together with selected video clips (for television) or audio clips (for radio). If a press kit has previously been assembled during production, an updated version will be used.

For films which originate from abroad, the publicist will usually use the press kits made by the international sales or foreign distribution company as a starting point. The materials will require adapting, and varying practices in different countries means that the publicist will often have to adapt materials. In France, for example, filmographies of cast and crew are preferred to biographies, so overseas publicists will have to create some material themselves.

These press kits will be distributed to the national and local press as well as television and radio journalists. They may also be sent to regional exhibitors for distribution to other local media and to help in their own campaigns.

THE IMPORTANCE OF STAR INTERVIEWS

The publicity generated by mainstream films is usually based around the stars and can be used to complement the advertising campaign. Such interviews can be pitched to newspapers or magazines as a means for them to increase their circulation.

On such mainstream pictures, the distributor should try to ensure that major stars undertake press tours, visiting as many territories where the film is to be released as possible, for interviews with the local media.

Alternatively, the stars can be made available for press junkets in which selected journalists and media are flown in to particular location for interviews with the stars. Such trips are often funded by the distributors themselves, since the resulting coverage is judged to justify the cost of flying in journalists.

The studios usually have greater leverage with the stars than other distributors because the stars often have long-term relationships with particular studio executives, or they may have an on-going production deal with a studio. The independents simply do not have these alliances, so they must be more inventive in order to secure the support of the talent in helping to promote the films to their potential audience.

For arthouse films, the publicity will focus on the creative aspect of the film or the director, if they are sufficiently well known. For instance, names such as Neil Jordan or Carlos Saura are sufficiently well known to support a publicity campaign. For unknown European talent or first-time directors, it is much harder to get media coverage, although in some cases the media like to discover new talent.

"If the media, especially in France, feel that a film made by relative unknowns is interesting, they are prepared to give it space," says French press agent Simona Benzakein. "In this way films like Les Nuits Fauves, Orlando or La Stazione can get the same treatment as bigger titles."

Interviews with stars and directors are an asset to film promotion. Box-office returns are usually higher for films that have been promoted by the stars and the director in different territories, than for those which have not enjoyed such publicity.

The aim of all these approaches is to generate major features and news pieces about the film across a wide variety of media.

ORGANISING THE PRESS SCREENING

Press screenings are primarily aimed at journalists who wish to review the film, although they will also serve a useful secondary function of spreading word of mouth among the media. The screenings will often be held at preview theatres, which are small cinemas devoted to such events.

These screenings will need to be organised well in advance of the release of the film. This is because both the print and audio-visual media will have deadlines a considerable time before they are actually published.

This gap between the press deadline and the publication date is known as the *lead time*. The lead time of various types of publication will tend to vary as follows:

- For monthly magazines, it may be necessary to organise the screening as much as three months ahead of the film's release date if the magazine is to be able to include the film in the issue concurrent with the release of the film.

- For weekly publications screenings can be organised one month ahead of release.

- For daily publications, screenings can be organised as little as two to three days before the release of the film.

Therefore it is crucial to ensure that sufficient lead time is allowed for the various types of publications to file their reviews. For any one film there may be several press screenings aimed at each category of publication.

Timing is also critical. "If you show the film to the media at the wrong moment, they may write about it in a very different way than if you show it to them at a more effective time," says San Fu Maltha, managing director of Dutch independent distribution company Meteor Films. Some distributors may prefer to keep a film under wraps until the last possible moment to heighten the sense of the release as an event. This approach may also be used to avoid bad word of mouth spreading if they feel the film is likely to be poorly reviewed.

Radio and television stations will again work to their own different and specific deadlines in advance of the airing of their broadcasts, and so special screenings for these media must also be scheduled in by the publicist.

Another effective strategy is for the publicist to organise private screenings for two to three selected journalists from daily newspapers, to start generating some early favourable opinions, although the reviews may not appear until nearer the release date of the film. These opinion formers, who will be hand-picked by the publicist to try to ensure a positive reaction to the film, may influence both the general public and other journalists.

Even mainstream pictures with large advertising budgets can suffer heavily if the critics respond negatively to the film. In such cases, an effective advertising and publicity campaign may be the only chance to overcome, if only partially, the impact of bad reviews on the likely box-office performance of the film.

STRATEGIES FOR PROMOTIONAL CAMPAIGNS

PREVIEW SCREENINGS

Preview screenings are used to reinforce publicity and advertising activities. As they are designed to ensure that word of mouth peaks with the release of the film, they are held at any time from three weeks in advance to just a few days ahead of release. Such screenings are usually free or jointly promoted with local radio and newspapers which assist in giving away tickets.

In setting up preview screenings, it is important that the distributor identifies those opinion makers who will exercise the most powerful influence over specific target groups.

There are several different types of preview screening: those for targeted groups of people organised in conjunction with sponsors, those that feature appearances by the director and/or stars, and those that are arranged for backers of the film or other private companies which may be involved with the picture.

Many preview screenings will be aimed particularly at parts of the population which are felt to be among the core audience for the film and which will help to spread word of mouth among their peers. For instance, for a film like Cyrano de Bergerac, promotional screenings were aimed at colleges and schools, many of whom would be studying the original play. The screenings would also reach teachers whose colleagues might well have a strong interest in seeing a film using such classic material.

> **The primary goal of a preview (or talker) screening is to boost word of mouth on a film.**

The tickets for such screenings would be distributed directly to selected academic institutions. Independent distributors who organise preview screenings may also try to reach their audience by giving away tickets in conjunction with the media. Radio stations are often targeted in the case of films aimed at youthful audiences, because their listeners have the correct age profile for the film. Tickets to preview screenings will be given to the first listeners to call in and correctly answer some simple questions, usually tied to the theme of the film. This also helps the radio station attract listeners. Competitions in newspapers or weekly magazines are often used in the same way.

Screenings which are attended by the director or star can also be very effective both in generating interest among particular target audiences and among the media.

The practice of preview screening has developed rapidly in Europe in the last few years. It has always been used heavily by the subsidiaries of the US majors in Europe, who might hold up to 200 previews across the continent in the case of films for which they feel that the want to see is weak, perhaps because the subject matter is not likely to be of immediate appeal to European audiences (for example, A League of Their Own).

The US majors and the larger independent distributors are in a strong position to co-ordinate previews as they have easy access to screens, the financial resources to create additional prints and strong negotiating power with the media. For them, spending money on free screenings is part of an overall marketing strategy geared to building audience awareness and word of mouth, with the goal of maximising admissions in the opening days of the film.

Some smaller independent distributors are also increasingly using such screenings. However, previews are still shunned by other distributors who claim that they invariably reach the same target group whatever the type of film – that is, those people who enter competitions in newspapers or on the radio.

Once the film has opened, the distributor can usually tell very quickly from the box-office results if previews have generated word of mouth that has helped the film to perform well, since the first-week performance will invariably act as a good guide to the film's future grosses.

GALA PREMIERES

Gala premieres of a film are prestigious evenings where the cast, crew and guests are invited to see the film at a prestigious cinema a few days in advance of its release. The goal is to secure media coverage of the event and, by extension, increase awareness of the film among cinema goers.

But the presence of journalists, good photographers and television crews is essential, as they can make reports about the event in people magazines or gossip columns. In Spain, the UK and certain other European countries, a common practice is to invite royalty to major premieres, boosting the media profile of the event.

Premieres can greatly increase editorial coverage of a film but they tend to be very expensive and will therefore be confined to films with higher P&A budgets.

MERCHANDISING CAMPAIGNS

A merchandising campaign involves the use of products which can reinforce the image or identity of a film. This can range from something as simple as a T-shirt, to an interactive video game based on the film. For the creation of simple merchandising items, distributors might handle the merchandising themselves. With other items such as toys, the producer of the film will often license the rights to use certain motifs or characters from the film to an independent toy manufacturer or merchandise company.

Merchandising serves a two-fold purpose: it raises awareness of the film among its target audience and it also creates an additional revenue stream for the producer of the picture since the licensing of rights can be very lucrative. Such campaigns will usually be most effective in the case of mainstream pictures, although innovative merchandising may sometimes be effective in the case of more specialised titles.

Promotional campaigns for films from the US majors are increasingly associated with the merchandising of products derived from it. At the high-budget end of the market, the American blockbuster Jurassic Park (budgeted at $60 million (ECU54 million) with a $60 million marketing campaign) was launched internationally by distributor UIP with 100 tie-ins, from

> **" A merchandising campaign involves the use of products which can reinforce the image or identity of a film. "**

T-shirts and toys, to interactive video games all drawing on aspects of the film. European distributors are unlikely to be handling films which have such a large number of potential tie-ins, but the promotional campaign can still be very important.

When creating a merchandising campaign it is important to stay within the spirit of a particular film. The most common tie-ins are the publishing of the book on which a film is based and the launching of the soundtrack with a record company simultaneously with the opening of the film. Both these promotional elements will use the visual images of the poster campaign.

Music soundtrack tie-ins can be very important in broadening the awareness of a particular film among its core audience. Such tie-ins have become increasingly important for many theatrical films in the last few years. The benefit of a successful music tie-in is that the film promotes the music and the music promotes the film. Airplay for a particular track or album serves to maintain public awareness of the film from which it is taken. For example, Everything I Do by Bryan Adams, taken from the Warner Brothers film Robin Hood: Prince of Thieves, was number one for many weeks, in many countries, ensuring that the film (excerpts from which featured heavily in the song's promotional video) kept a high profile. A film soundtrack LP or CD also provides promotional material and prizes for competitions as well as potential point-of-sale displays in record shops, which are targeted predominantly at the 15-24 age group.

Joint promotions with shops or department stores, in which shop windows are arranged to evoke a scene or character from a film in the week preceding its release, can also be exploited. This approach can be used for many different types of film. For example in France, the independent distribution company MK2 worked in conjunction with the department store Printemps to create window displays based on the film Madame Bovary.

The development of interactive media is likely to lead to an increase in the potential number of licensing and merchandising opportunities. For instance, it is likely that in the future many more interactive games may be based upon characters derived from a film. Even the growth of virtual reality technology presents an opportunity for film makers to licence their characters for use in entertainment-based games. The US majors are already exploring the possibilities in such areas, but independents could also benefit from the openings which may arise.

SPONSORSHIP

As with tie-ins and promotions, distributors are increasingly turning to sponsorship as a means of offsetting their P&A costs. In a promotional campaign such as a record or book tie-in, the distributor will receive the respective merchandise in return for joint promotions. By contrast, sponsorship entails the distributor receiving financial assistance or airplay in return for branding a particular sponsor's logo onto the film's advertising and promotional material. Such material could include posters, trailers,

KEY POINTS OF PUBLICITY AND PROMOTION

THE PRESS KIT
- Press kits should include cast and crew credits, production notes, stills and biographies and filmographies of the cast, director and producer. The electronic press kit will contain many of the same items together with selected video clips (for television) or audio clips (for radio).

STAR INTERVIEWS
- Can be pitched to newspapers or magazines as a means for them to increase their circulation, and to give the film free publicity.

THE PRESS SCREENING
- Primarily aimed at journalists who wish to review the film, although they will also serve a useful secondary function of spreading word of mouth among the media. The screenings should be organised well in advance of release.

PREVIEW SCREENINGS
- To boost word of mouth on the film. Word of mouth, the passage of opinion on a film from one person to another, has a key impact on the performance of a picture.

MERCHANDISING CAMPAIGNS
- Involves the use of products which feature certain aspects of the film. This can range from something as simple as a T-shirt featuring the logo of a film, or an interactive video game based on the film.

brochures and clothing such as jackets or caps.

Sponsorship will invariably come from companies manufacturing consumer durables seeking the same audience demographic as a particular film, or companies seeking to raise their profile. As an example of the latter, on the film 1492, Christopher Columbus, the film's French distribution company Gaumont secured sponsorship from the bank Le Crédit Agricole, which co-financed the whole advertising campaign. The bank also organised competitions such as awarding a prize for the Crédit Agricole branch featuring the best display based on the film. In total the French bank invested Fr4 million (ECU593,431) in the campaign and in return received a mention in the film's credits.

Having examined the ways in which the distributor creates a strategy for marketing and advertising the film, it is now time to look at the role of the exhibitor in marketing the film.

EXHIBITION IN EUROPE

" The marketing effort should not end with the distributor. The exhibitor can also play a key role in helping to promote the film to the public. **"**

The cinema operator, also known as the exhibitor, is the key link between a film and its target audience. While the distributor's task is to persuade the public to pay to see a particular film, exhibitors must persuade the audience to see the film at their own cinema. The distributor and exhibitor will work together closely to create a marketing strategy to achieve these goals. This section will examine the strategies used by the cinema operators to ensure that they maximise their revenues.

DECLINING STANDARDS, FALLING ADMISSIONS

Until the mid-1980s, cinema circuits in many countries, notably Germany, Italy and the UK, had received little in the way of investment, and as a consequence many cinemas fell into a state of disrepair, with poor seating and low-quality screens a feature of some cinemas. This applied primarily to the cinemas owned by the large chains, although it was equally applicable to some independent or arthouse cinemas.

Attendance levels in many European countries had plummeted, yet few exhibitors apparently made the causal connection with the poor state of some cinemas, preferring to blame the growth of ancillary media such as television or video for the rapid decline in the popularity of the big screen.

Management standards were often poor both at a national level and within individual cinemas. Few cinemas had the ability to take credit card bookings from customers, the range of concessions was limited and standards of cleanliness were low. The only major territory that was an exception to this rule was France, where the vitality of the domestic cinema industry and the keen interest shown by the French public in films meant that the major chains such as Gaumont, UGC and Pathé had maintained a programme of continuous investment in maintaining their cinemas.

Among those suffering most heavily from this decline in admissions were the Hollywood distributors, since their revenues were falling in some territories. As a result, the US majors took the lead in the move to rejuvenate the European exhibition industry.

THE INTRODUCTION OF THE MULTIPLEX

The multiplex, a common type of cinema in the US, typically comprises 8 to 10 screens and is located on the edge of a city or large conurbation with easy road access. Such cinemas are often located close to large shopping centres, which offer easy access for cars and the possibility of combining a visit to the cinema with another activity such as shopping or eating out.

Inside, the cinema usually features a wide range of concessions, and frequently houses a restaurant and bar. The seats are much wider and more comfortable than those found inside older cinemas. Advance booking and credit card booking are both available.

Each of the auditoria will have a different seating capacity, appropriate to different types of film, ranging from mainstream blockbusters to smaller arthouse pictures. A mainstream film can also be moved to one of the smaller auditoria once it has been running for several weeks and audience interest starts to wane. Moving the film to another cinema in this way – a process known as *moveover* – prolongs its run, ensuring that box-office revenues are maximised.

Starting times of the films are usually staggered, so that if customers cannot get in to the film of their choice because it is full, they have the choice of attending other films, which start within a short space of time. Each auditorium will have up to five screenings a day.

The pioneer in multiplex building in the EC countries was Belgium's Bert family. With three generations of cinema exhibitors before him and the desire to offer audiences the same comfort as they might find in their own homes but with better sound (digital) and better visibility (70mm prints), Albert Bert began the transformation of a one-screen cinema into a triplex in 1972. He ended up building with another family (Claeys) what was to become the biggest multi-screen complex in Europe: the Kinepolis. The 25-screen complex has had an enormous impact on admissions in Brussels: today it attracts more than 3 million people a year and has a 55% market share in the city.

In the UK, American Multi-Cinema (AMC) was the first to introduce multiplexes with the development of a site in Milton Keynes, north of London, in 1985. The subsequent boom in multiplex building enabled the UK to be the only country within the EC to register a net increase in box-office admissions over the last 8 years.

The American chains have also invested considerable time in training their local managers, in an effort to improve relations with their customers. For example, United Cinemas International

(UCI) sends all its managers to a Training Academy which it has established in Manchester, in the north of England. Each quarter, a new batch of managers is sent for 4 to 6 weeks of classroom work which examines all aspects of the cinema industry, with specific emphasis on marketing cinemas to the public. Once they have completed their work, the managers are put into a cinema and their progress is evaluated on a quarterly basis.

Many other European groups, such as Rank in UK, Flebbe Filmtheater in Germany, UGC, Gaumont and Pathé in France and Penta in Italy, are involved in multiplex building and cinema refurbishment as a means of staying competitive.

ARTHOUSE CINEMAS

While the multiplex cinema has been the main engine of growth in the European exhibition sector, arthouse cinemas have also played a role in driving up attendances. Arthouses predominantly show specialised, niche films (often of European origin), although some houses do screen more mainstream pictures, as a means of maintaining a certain level of admissions. The majority of these cinemas throughout Europe tend to be independently owned.

In the last 10 years, many arthouse operators in Europe have spent money on refurbishing these cinemas in the face of competition from new multiplex operators, as well as from the established chains which have been revamping their circuits.

In order to compete with the multiplexes, the arthouse cinemas must not only show a different type of film but must also provide a different type of experience.

For instance, realising that many spectators are irked by cinema commercials, the screens owned by the independent Alta Films in Spain do not carry advertising, a policy which is common to many independents throughout Europe.

Other arthouse cinemas will offer facilities such as a café or restaurant or the installation of a bookshop.

"Our café facilities not only generate extra revenue, they also create a certain atmosphere that should help attract customers," says Peter Refn, owner of the Grand, a leading arthouse cinema in Copenhagen, and also a key arthouse distributor in Denmark. Such cafés are an increasingly common feature of independent cinemas around Europe, and may even be open to people who are not going to see a film but are using it as a meeting place. In many cases, the cafés will offer a full meal, with an emphasis on health food likely to appeal to the more liberal tastes of the prospective audience. As a consequence, there is less reliance on the sales of concessions such as popcorn and hot dogs.

The internal decoration of the cinema may also be geared towards a more selective audience. The restaurant space at the Grand Cinema is decorated with film memorabilia, creating surroundings which are likely to appeal to an educated audience with an appreciation of cinema history. Some cinemas will stock film books designed to enhance the sense of cinematic tradition, but which may provide a useful source of additional revenue.

Traditionally, most arthouse cinemas have relied heavily on arthouse pictures. But in the face of the increasing share of the European box office which is being snared by US films, many independents have had to adopt a more varied programming diet in order to remain viable. While art films – predominantly but not exclusively European in origin – still tend to form the backbone of programming for the independents, many have started to show selected "quality" films from Hollywood. "Our cinemas are playing more American films than in the past," says Andi Engel, director of Artificial Eye, which operates independent screens in London and is also involved in distribution.

THE IMPORTANCE OF CONCESSIONS AND SCREEN ADVERTISING

For both multiplexes and arthouse cinemas, box-office receipts alone are sometimes insufficient to give the exhibitor a profit. Screen advertising, shown prior to the start of the film, and sales of concessions such as confectionery and soft drinks, offer a lucrative source of additional revenue.

Concessions may represent as much as 20-25% of total profit in some European cinemas and so maximising revenues from concession sales is a priority for most exhibitors. One reason why income from concessions is so high is that the margins on food and drink sold in cinemas may be as high as 60%.

The sale of advertising is usually handled either by the chain itself or by an independent sales house. Advertising provides a boost to the income of the cinema chains, but there is concern among some producers and distributors that excessive amounts of advertising may deter audiences. Several chains in Europe have introduced limitations on the amount of advertising they carry, although the economic importance of screen advertising makes many exhibitors reluctant to pursue such a policy.

Screen advertisers can be either independent or connected to a cinema chain – for example, Rank Screen Advertising is linked to Rank's Odeon cinema chain in the UK. Each European country has two to three major groups that sell screen advertising (see chart).

> " For both multiplexes and arthouse cinemas, box-office receipts alone are sometimes insufficient to give the exhibitor a profit. "

MARKETING STRATEGIES

BOOKING

If distributors are to maximise the chances of a film performing well at the cinema, they must maintain good relationships with the film bookers who work for the cinema chains, and are responsible for booking the films into the cinemas for a specified period of time.

Some chains will have one national booker, supplemented by a number of regional bookers who will have responsibility for a particular local area. The regional bookers are in constant contact with local cinema managers who relay information about audience reaction to certain types of film, or particular stars. In the case of smaller chains or independent cinemas, it will often be the managing director or owner of the company who personally takes responsibility for booking the films.

Although bookers will generally be willing to book big-name films without seeing them, few will be prepared to take this risk on smaller, more specialised pictures. In the case of most mainstream pictures, the film will be booked three to six months in advance although major US blockbusters will be booked up to a year in advance of their release.

> **There is concern among some producers and distributors that excessive amounts of advertising may act as a deterrent to audiences.**

Booking the film less than three months ahead usually leaves insufficient time to prepare fully the marketing campaign for a film, but nevertheless it is common practice, particularly in the case of smaller films.

In some smaller countries even large cinema chains tend to book most of their films just two months in advance of release.

After viewing the film, the exhibitor will meet with the distributor to discuss the release pattern. In some cases, the distributor may have to exert pressure on the exhibitor, because the latter may be reluctant to take a certain number of prints or to offer particular screens. This is particularly the case with specialised pictures, because exhibitors are often unwilling to take risks on such films. They will offer such films unattractive opening dates, or may offer playdates at very short notice, allowing too little time for the development of an effective marketing campaign.[1]

Equally, the exhibitor may also face problems when negotiating with the distributor. The practice of block booking, under which larger distributors will only guarantee a cinema chain their hit

---

1 See Section Five: Film Distribution in Europe.

Key cinema advertising houses in Europe

AD HOUSES   **SCREENS**

Belgium	Cinéma Publicitaire Belge	217
	Vadam KH	142
Denmark	Dansk Reklame Film	276
	Bergenholz Film	276
France	Médiavision	2,289
	Circuit A	770
Germany	UFA Werbefilm GmbH	2,600
	DECO	675
	Union-Werbeverwaltung GmbH	405
	Heinefilm Walter Kelemant Werbung GmbH	385
	Kinomatfilm A Limbergwerbe GmbH	318
	Ancora Werbung GmbH	288
	Udia Fimverbung Franz Schönlecokg	246
	Wolf-Werbung GmbH	228
	Europa Film & Werbung	192
	Wegra Werbung GmbH	156
Greece	Cine News Ltd	221
	Kronos	152
Ireland	Rank Screen Advertising	173
Italy	Sipra	530
	Opus Proclama	307
Netherlands	Cloek en Moedigh	243
	Cinescope Blooscoopreklame BV	193
Portugal	Belate	85
	Ecran	52
Spain	Movierecord	1,291
	Distel	530
	Cinexclusivas	188
	Vinoco Ortega	14
UK	Rank Screen Advertising	1,309
	Pearl & Dean	347

source : 1992 European Cinema Minibook, Carat

titles if they also agree to book some weaker or less successful pictures, is privately acknowledged as a constant problem for exhibitors in some territories, although few are willing publicly to denounce the practice. However, there is little that the exhibitors can do to resist the policy of block booking since the larger distributors control the supply of the hit films which are the lifeblood of most cinema chains.

Because delivery times of films are often subject to change, bookers are constantly having to revise the opening dates for films. However, arthouse exhibitors tend to be more rigid in their booking policy. They will usually book a film for a minimum period of four to six weeks, and as long as the takings exceed the house nut, it will not be taken off to make way for another picture.

DISTRIBUTORS WHO ARE ALSO EXHIBITORS

One advantage for distributors who are also exhibitors is, in most instances, their ability to book their own films for preferred dates. Since in many of the European markets there is a shortage of screens, many distributors, especially the smaller companies, often have to wait a considerable amount of time before they can open their films.

The distributor who owns cinemas also has the singular advantage of being able to control the hold-over of films, keeping titles on screen rather longer than an exhibitor might do in normal circumstances.

The respective goals of distributor and exhibitor are often in conflict. If a film records a satisfactory box office in the first week of release and the critics subsequently review it, receipts will often rise slightly and then start going down, although there are still people who will go and see it because they simply didn't have time during the first and second weekend.

The exhibitor makes money in the first four weeks while the distributor has only just paid for prints and for subtitling by that stage, and only starts to make money after that. In many cases, therefore, the exhibitor would like to have a new film at the point at which the distributor is only just starting to make money.

> "The respective goals of distributor and exhibitor are often in conflict."

So while both the distributor and the exhibitor wish to see a film gross the maximum amount of revenue possible, the time frame in which they wish to achieve this goal is somewhat different. Clearly, such a situation has the potential to create conflict between the two sides.

WORKING WITH THE EXHIBITOR TO MARKET THE FILM

Distributors should try to ensure that their own marketing effort is supplemented by similar efforts on the part of the exhibitors, in order to give the film the best possible chance of maximising its target audience.

The distributor of the film will be responsible for handling the trailer, the poster and any television advertising campaign. Few exhibitors will have direct input into the construction of these campaigns, although in some countries they will be asked to bear some of the cost of the prints and advertising. In Switzerland, for instance, exhibitors are expected to fund 50% of the costs of local advertising equivalent to 10-15% of the entire P&A budget.

However, the marketing effort should not end with the distributor. The exhibitor can also play a key role in helping to promote the film to the public. The most common form of marketing that the exhibitor will undertake is to buy space in the local newspapers to advertise the films they are screening. These advertisements will often appear on the day of the film's change over – often a Friday – as many chains will do anywhere from 30-60% of their business during the weekend period. Only in very rare instances will the exhibitor use television advertising as the price is simply too prohibitive.

Many cinema chains try to ensure that the local managers of each cinema in the group are in close contact with the local media, in the two months leading up to the release of the film. The manager will be asked to prepare a marketing plan for their cinema for a picture, based on a specific marketing hook.

" Involving local exhibitors in the promotion of the film can pay handsome dividends. "

If any aspect of the picture has a local hook – for example, the film's content may relate in some way to the local area – this can be used to maximise the marketing potential of the film. The aim of the campaign will be to convey information about the date or time when the film will screen, while also giving the public a flavour of the individual title.

The marketing plan may involve identifying certain key sites for advertising the film, or creating a competition in partnership with a local paper or retail store in which tickets to see the film are given away. This will ensure editorial coverage of the film in the local paper. The goal of the plan is simple – to maximise awareness of the film and stimulate want to see.

On larger productions, some chains may invite all their cinema managers to a talk given by the star or director of the specific film. Such events will also provide an opportunity for the managers to be photographed with the star or the director, providing useful publicity material for the local media.

Involving local exhibitors in the promotion of the film can pay handsome dividends. In the run-up to the release in France of 1492, Christopher Columbus, Gaumont organised a competition between exhibitors throughout the country. The exhibitor to have set up the most original and attractive campaign to promote the film won a free trip to Spain. "We just wanted to motivate the exhibitors and the promotion had a big impact on the local press and audience," says Arnaud de Rouvillois, formerly marketing director for Gaumont.

MORE GENERAL FORMS OF MARKETING

There are a number of other, more general strategies which may be used by the exhibitor to promote both specific films and the idea of cinema going in general. Wherever possible, the distributor should seek to encourage the exhibitor to explore the possibility of such promotions since they will benefit both parties.

One form of marketing frequently undertaken by the cinema chains themselves is the production of a magazine or newsletter which gives information about forthcoming releases. Such publications are usually glossy, four-colour productions, financed by advertising and distributed in the cinema foyer to patrons of the cinema. In some instances, the chains may charge a cover price for such publications.

Some exhibitors are starting to explore generic promotion of the idea of cinema going as a strategy to boost admissions. Campaigns can include the use of slogans encouraging people to go to the cinema, on posters and on other merchandise such as sweatshirts, in an attempt to convince the public that the cinema is the primary medium for film.

Promotional initiatives such as the Fête du Cinéma held in France in late June and the Festa del Cinema in Italy in May/June, when cinemas offer discount price tickets for an extended period, are also proving successful both in raising attendances during a specific period and in raising the profile of cinema going as a whole. This also provides an opportunity for the public to meet with members of the film industry. Some exhibitors organise mini-festivals designed to promote certain types of film. During the summer, the Kinepolis complex in Belgium organises a week-long festival during which they premiere particular titles from Europe and the US.

The goal of generic promotions is often to attract people who seldom visit the cinema or who do not consider cinema going as a potential leisure activity. In an attempt to attract older audiences, the Svenskfilmindustri chain in Sweden sells cinema tickets to large companies which it can give away to employees. Such people tend to be older than the 15-25 age group which constitutes the core cinema-going group.

UCI in the UK has made strenuous attempts to attract those aged 35+ into the cinemas by offering such facilities as advanced seat booking, credit card booking, as well as by ensuring that each location offers a broad range of programming. As a result of these efforts the demographic of the British cinema goer has broadened slightly, since before the multiplexes were introduced the audience overwhelmingly fell into the 15-25 age bracket.

The MGM Group in The Netherlands has created various strategies for reaching particular niche groups. On some Sunday mornings during the winter, the company programmes dance films in key city cinemas, and invites dance schools and others to attend.

Other European exhibitors, especially arthouse chains, use direct marketing to reach potential customers. They often send out programmes detailing forthcoming films, and some cinemas keep a database of their customers (constructed from the credit card records) and mail them with information on screenings on a regular basis. Direct marketing allows cinemas to market to particular types of audience for particular types of film, providing a highly effective means of targeting certain groups.

THE ROLE OF TICKET PRICING

The different forms of ticket pricing can also be used by the exhibitor as a means to encourage the public into the cinema. The most popular innovation in ticket pricing in recent years has been the introduction of a particular day each week when ticket prices for the public are reduced across the board. This increases the competitiveness of cinema going as compared with other leisure activities.

Such discounts are used both by the large chains and by the smaller independent cinemas. The day when the discount is offered varies widely across Europe. For example, Kinepolis in Belgium offers cheaper tickets on Monday, while Flebbe Filmtheater in Germany makes its discounts on Wednesday. In France, Wednesday is discount day for every cinema.

The rate of discount offered usually varies between 20-30%, depending on the individual chain. Aside from the weekend period, the discount day usually accounts for the largest volume of business. For instance, Flebbe Filmtheater does 15% of its business on discount day, a much higher level than on any other weekday except Friday.

" " The most popular innovation in ticket pricing in recent years has been the introduction of a particular day each week when prices are reduced across the board. " "

In France, this concept has been taken further with entire weeks given over to discounted ticket sales. During such discount weeks, Pathé Cinéma, for example, sells tickets at Fr20 (ECU2.55/$2.84), against an average price of Fr40.

In many Italian cinemas discounts on tickets are offered on Wednesdays, but since the policy is not applied uniformly by all exhibitors it has been less effective in attracting large-scale audiences into the cinema on that day.

Many chains are also paying increasing attention to the optimum price of a ticket for maximising their audience in the face of competition from other leisure pursuits.[2]

Average cinema ticket prices in EC countries and North America
(figures in US dollars)

	1985	1990	1991	1992
Belgium	2.62	4.90	4.77	4.97
Denmark	2.49	4.80	4.54	5.18
France	3.30	6.12	6.05	6.85
Germany	3.02	5.41	4.89	5.74
Greece	1.35	4.03	6.45	5.55
Ireland	3.86	4.30	4.29	4.53
Italy	2.42	5.92	5.92	7.14
Neth'nds	3.66	6.80	6.47	7.29
Portugal	1.02	2.62	2.65	3.29
Spain	1.62	3.72	3.72	4.66
UK	2.46	4.79	4.71	5.99
EC average	2.60	5.21	5.10	6.00
Canada	2.92	4.65	4.68	4.49
US	3.55	4.75	4.96	5.05

source : Screen Digest

The chart left shows that the average cost of a cinema ticket in EC countries was lower than that of the US in 1985. But the average price of tickets in EC countries more than doubled between 1985 and 1990, so that the average ticket is now more expensive than in the US.

2 "Targeting the 15-24-year-old age range, we had to get the British audience out of the pubs and into the cinemas, away from couch potato and video potato syndrome, ...giving them what they wanted, a good service and value for money. So we aimed the ticket price at the price of two pints of beer, about £4.00." Charles Wesoky, former chief executive, UCI, quoted in Screen International, April 9th 1993.

THE IMPORTANCE OF TRAILERS

Once the audience is inside the cinema, the screening of trailers can be a very effective way of persuading them to return to see forthcoming films. Here the distributor must work as closely as possible with the exhibitor to ensure that the impact of the trailer is maximised, since many cinemas are reluctant to play trailers as, unlike screen advertising, they do not offer an immediate source of income.[3] As a result, as much as 75% of the time before the screening of a film will be given over to advertising and only 25% to trailers. This only allows enough time for two or three trailers to be shown.

However, the under-utilisation of trailers is not purely the fault of the exhibitor. The length of many contemporary films creates problems. It is frequently difficult to show a sufficiently varied number of trailers, because the films are getting longer and longer. Ten years ago the average length of a film was 90 minutes, now it is closer to 120 minutes. Since the film has to be screened a certain number of times each day, the time available for trailers may well be cut.

But the exhibitors want to strike the right balance between attracting the audience to future presentations and maintaining its appetite for the film which they have paid to see. As a result some chains deliberately restrict the length of time for which they will show trailers. In Holland, for example, MGM has cut the length of the advertising and trailers from 28 minutes (15 minutes of commercials and 13 minutes of trailers) to 15 minutes (10 minutes of commercials and 5 minutes of trailers), after market research revealed that 60% of cinema customers thought the advertising/trailer period was too long. Few European exhibitors now play more than 10 minutes of trailers before a film.

> " The timing of the delivery of trailers is imperative with regard to securing maximum impact with audiences. "

Ideally, a trailer for a film should start being shown two months before its release, yet some exhibitors complain that distributors deliver the trailer to the exhibitor with just four weeks to go.

This often means that the potential audience will only see the trailer once or twice before the film is released. As a result, much of the impact of the trailer as a marketing tool will be completely lost on the cinema goer.

The timing of the delivery of trailers is imperative with regard to securing maximum impact with audiences. Ideally, the distributor should deliver the trailers to the exhibitor at least six weeks before the release of the film to allow sufficient time for it to be exposed

3 Compared with the US where there is no screen advertising and the emphasis is firmly on trailers.

to the audience on a regular basis, and to create a mood of expectation. Teaser trailers should be delivered two to three months in advance of the film's release.

Because of this reluctance by exhibitors to spend too much time showing trailers, their length becomes critical. The shorter they are, the more likely the exhibitor is to screen them. In many cases, shorter trailers are also more likely to have an impact with the cinema-going audience. For both these reasons a sharp, punchy 30-second trailer that singles out a few dramatic moments in the film could be much more effective than a three-minute version which attempts to encapsulate the entire story.[4]

However, there are signs in some European territories of attempts to use trailers in more innovative ways. Some cinema chains have realised that the value of trailers may not be measured in immediate income to the bottom line, but that they nevertheless draw people into the cinema over the long term.

As such some exhibitors, Cinema 5 in Italy for example, have introduced strategies designed to make more effective use of trailers. The company has devised a scheme in which distributors would create a package of five trailers, each of one minute in duration, which would play in 800 cinemas across the country. This package will play in addition to the normal three minutes of trailers shown by each exhibitor. The underlying philosophy is simple: ensure that trailers are shown to the maximum number of people possible, in an attempt to instil a regular cinema-going habit in those who visit the cinema.

In addition to screening trailers in the usual way, Germany's Flebbe Filmtheater has also installed walls of TV screens showing trailers in the lobby. The concept of free weekly trailer shows, to give the audience a foretaste of coming attractions, is also being used by a number of cinema chains.

REPORTING

Once a film has opened each cinema chain must make a regular and detailed report to the distributor of the money earned by the film at individual cinemas. This process is called *reporting* and should be very closely monitored by the distributor. Accuracy is

4 See section on Trailers above p.136/7.

vital as the reporting process will form the basis of allocating the revenues between the exhibitor, the distributor, the producer and any other parties (such as the star or the director) who may have an equity interest in the film.

It is in the opening days of a film, and particularly the opening weekend, when reporting is particularly critical, since this is the first opportunity for both distributor and cinema chain to assess the likely run of a given film in a given territory. If the film has already opened in another country, this may provide some indication of likely performance.

> **" It is not until the exhibitor reveals the opening figures for the film that an informed forecast of its likely performance can be made. "**

The reviews of the film, which will usually have been published just a few days before the release of the picture, may also offer a clue to the film's potential appeal to the public. But it is not until the exhibitor reveals the opening figures for the film that an informed forecast of its likely performance can be made. As films invariably perform most strongly in their opening week, and admissions gradually decrease from the second week onwards, it is possible to extrapolate considerable information from these opening figures.

In the opening week of a film most cinemas will report their gross box office to the distributor on a daily basis. These figures will be sent by fax or telephoned through to the distributor. Some distributors, such as Monopole-Pathé in Switzerland, operate a dedicated line with answerphone attached, so that exhibitors can phone in the results after the last performance of the day. In subsequent weeks, reporting will most often be done on a weekly basis. In some countries such as Belgium, Germany and Sweden, one group, acting on behalf of the distributors, is responsible for collecting all the box-office information and disseminating it.

The advantage of using such independent groups to collect the box-office information is that it becomes much harder for the various parties involved to consistently distort figures, since the collection group will have a detailed knowledge of the grosses achieved by individual cinemas.

The reports that are filed by the exhibitor will form the basis for calculating the box-office share to each party. The percentage of the gross that is returned to the distributor is known as the net rental share.

Before calculating the distributor's share of the box-office gross, the cinema operator first deducts its expenses from the total gross. Clearly, the costs of running cinemas vary widely, and will depend on location, the number of screens, labour costs and several other factors.

The net rental share varies widely across Europe. For example, in Germany net rentals have increased over the last 10 years from around 40-42% of the box office in the first four weeks of a film's release to 45-50%. In part, this reflects the fact that the distributor has been bearing an increased share of the marketing cost of films relative to the exhibitor. But by the end of the film's run, the distributor may be taking as little as 30% of the total gross.

SUPPORT MECHANISMS FOR EUROPEAN EXHIBITORS

Alongside local state subsidies to cinemas, in some countries, a number of publicly funded initiatives have also been founded to assist European exhibitors in their marketing efforts, particularly with regard to the screening of European films. The two most prominent of these organisations are Europa Cinémas and Media Salles.

EUROPA CINÉMAS

Europa Cinémas is an initiative of the EC MEDIA Programme which has the support of the CNC (The French national film body) and Eureka Audiovisuel. Its aim is to support those European cinemas that programme at least 51% European films. These cinemas will be situated in the capitals or in key European cities and will be part of a network called Pavilion Theatres.

Europa Cinémas will contribute up to 50% of the costs of cinema promotion (with a maximum of ECU30,000 per cinema each year) and the exhibitor is expected to provide the other 50%. For instance, in The Netherlands, the programme funded 50% of the costs of producing a special brochure dedicated to European films which was distributed in all Dutch cinemas.

However, the funds cannot be used for capital investment in equipment such as digital sound systems. The main objective is to support the release of new European films but in order to preserve the "memory" of European cinema, retrospectives organised by exhibitors can also benefit from Europa Cinémas' financial help. In the long term, Europa Cinémas wants to see more involvement by European stars and directors in promoting their films at individual cinemas.

KEY POINTS

BOOKING	• Films will generally be booked three to six months in advance. Distributors may need to press hard for preferred dates and screens in the case of specialised films. Arthouse cinemas will generally have a more rigid booking policy.
MARKETING BY THE EXHIBITOR	• Should be encouraged to promote the film using local media and retailers. Can use competitions to give away tickets. Arthouses may use direct marketing to reach regular customers.
TICKET PRICING	• Discounting of ticket prices on a regular basis is a highly effective way of attracting customers to the cinema.
DELIVERY OF PROMOTIONAL MATERIAL	• Distributor must ensure that they are delivered to exhibitors at least four weeks in advance, and that they are then played regularly.
REPORTING	• The distributor must monitor the process carefully to ensure the accuracy of returns.

MEDIA SALLES The goals of Media Salles include helping exhibitors in their promotional efforts and assisting in the training of industry professionals in the exhibition section, particularly with regard to marketing strategies. It is based in Italy, and funded by the MEDIA Programme in collaboration with the Italian Ministry for Tourism and Entertainment.

Media Salles also devised the week of European cinema, in which it supported the screening of European films by some 100 exhibitors, undertaking to cover up to 50% of the costs of organisational and promotional expenses of participating cinemas.

APPENDIX

GLOSSARY

INDEX

AUTHORS' BIOGRAPHIES

LIFESTAGES OF A FILM

The lifestages of a film can be broken down into six main sections which are detailed below. This breakdown is intended to act as a guide to the various stages which a film may pass through, although the pattern may vary for each individual film, and not all stages may be applicable. A different marketing strategy will be used at each step. Steps one to four deal with selling the film to the industry; step five deals with theatrical distribution and step six with ancillary rights.

How and when to implement the marketing plan will depend on the type of film being made, what is perceived to be the optimum time to initiate and conclude sales and, of course, the actual response to the film as it is being made and when it is completed.

1 – PRE-PRODUCTION

Idea (existing/adaptation)

Development

Treatment

Script (drafts)

Financing

Possible pre-sales

Positioning elements
- Introduction to targeted buyers/distributors
- Introduction to general trade (e.g. exhibitors, festivals etc)
- Through trade press announcements, industry events

Preliminary image

2 – PRODUCTION

Further financing

Pre-sales to commence (script and package elements to key buyers)

Introduction to further buyers

Preliminary image (if not commenced in pre-production stage)

Stills, footage, showreel may be produced to assist in sales

3 – POST PRODUCTION

Showreel (if not produced above)

Trailer (commence production of)

Visual or poster

Festival selections

Pre-sales based on above to continue and/or building word of mouth

4 – COMPLETED

Screening completed film

Festival, market, or other platform

Positioning to industry and public
- Distributors, response
- Critics, response
- Refine image, trailer

Prepare to deliver to distributors

5 – IN DISTRIBUTION MARKETING TO THE PUBLIC/ COMPLETE SALES

Festival platform to consider

Release in its domestic territory;

What effect will it have on other territories, especially those not yet sold?

Release in other European territories

In the US

Marketing parameters
- Audience/critics, reaction
- Festival response
- Other films' performance
- Cast's performance in other films

6 - OTHER MEDIA

How will theatrical release effect eventual sale to ancillary markets, video, television?

If already sold, how will theatrical release effect video revenue (i.e number of videos rented or sold) and value to future television sales?

GLOSSARY

Advertorial: a combination of advertising and editorial in which a publication runs copy promoting a film, (e.g. a competition or supplied text). The space is normally bought as media space or bought by supplying goods in kind, such as competition prizes.

Ancillary markets: (also called secondary or non-theatrical markets): the markets which are supplementary to the theatrical market. It includes home video, free-TV and pay-TV.

Announcing ad: the first advertisement placed in the film trade publications to announce the start or completion of the principal photography or any information concerning a film.

Arthouse: a concept synonym for specialised films often, but not always, made outside the Hollywood system by independent producers around the world. They appeal to targeted audiences in each territory although some of them might have a cross-over potential.

Avid cinema goer: the cinephile who goes to the cinema at least once a fortnight and who will be highly influential in spreading word of mouth on a film.

Awareness: one of the feelings which a distributor has to create among the target audience so that it knows that the film is being released, and has some idea of its most appealing elements.

Block-booking: a practice under which large distribution companies guarantee exhibitors a supply of mainstream films only if they agree to play less desirable titles.

Booker: the individual responsible for booking the films into the cinemas at a certain date. The film booker works for a film distribution company or a cinema circuit. Also known as the sales manager or programmer.

Break-even: the point when the distributor recoups their investment in a film. This will usually consist of their minimum guarantee and the P&A spend.

Bumper issues: special editions published by the film trade magazines just before the start of a market. They comprise listings of the sales companies with their films on sale, as well as general analyses of the market trends.

Buzz: slang for good word-of-mouth, or positive gossip on a film.

Change over day: the opening or release day of a film.

Cold selling: the potential buyer is contacted for the first time without a prior introduction to the material being sold.

Completion guarantee: a form of insurance for the financiers of a film designed to protect them in the event of the film running over budget. The guarantor provides a bond guaranteeing that the film will be delivered on time, on budget and to the distributor's requirements. The producer has to pay a fee in return for the security offered by the guarantor.

Costs off the top: part of the distribution equation whereby a distributor deducts costs from the net rental (i.e. gross box office less exhibitor's share) and then their distribution fee. Any remaining profits would then be remitted as overages, according to a previously agreed formula with the producer and/or the sales agent.

Counter-programming: the decision to open a film against another title of a different genre in order to offer a distinct alternative to the audience.

Cross-collateralisation: used for rights or territories. The cross-collateralisation of rights means that the distributor offsets any losses from a film incurred from the theatrical market against profits from sales in other markets such as TV or video before distributing the share of the profits to the sales agent and the producer. The cross-collateralisation of territories is commonly used by the Hollywood studios. The studio will seek to cross-collateralise profits and losses between territories so that the producer will only be entitled to a share of the profits from a specific territory once the combined profits of the film outweigh the combined losses.

Cross-over film: a film originally targeted for a specialised audience which succeeds in attracting a broader audience.

Dailies: refers to trade publications which are produced daily at the main film markets and festivals, Cannes, the AFM and MIFED. This term can also refer to Variety and the Hollywood Reporter, both of which produce daily editions throughout the year.

Day and date release: a wide-opening release when a film opens simultaneously in a large number of cinemas nationwide.

Delivery: this constitutes supplying defined elements such as a print in original version, legal agreements, artwork or publicity material. Payments made from distributors to sales agents or producers usually become payable upon delivery.

Discounting: the practice of advancing funds to a producer against the value of distribution or pre-sales contracts. Interest will be charged by the financial lender.

Distributor: any person responsible for the buying of rights to films for the theatrical, television and/or video market. The distributor is the link between the producer and the exhibitor to ensure that the producer's films are shown in the various media. Another key role played by the distributor involves collecting film revenues and distributing them to the various people involved in the financing of the film. The distributor is usually responsible for the marketing and promotion of the film.

Double-page spreads: an advertisement taken in a trade publication which is spread over two pages.

Electronic Press Kit (EPK): the audio or video version of a films' promotional materials sent to radio and television stations. It will contain many of the items contained in the printed press kit together with audio or video interviews with the directors or the main cast.

Equity investors: any person or company wishing to invest in a production in return for a share of the eventual profits.

Executive producer: one of the individuals responsible for obtaining the financing for a film; can also be involved in the creative process of the production.

Exhibitor: the owner or operator of a cinema.

Feature print: a full-length film print which is usually 90-180 minutes in length.

First look: in a production deal with a US studio, the latter provides development money to an independent producer on the grounds that they will have first refusal to invest in any project that comes to fruition, in return for certain distribution rights.

Flyposting: the activity of putting posters unofficially on walls and buildings.

Focus groups: groups of people surveyed during market research to assess the likely performance of different films prior to their release.

Gross deal: a distribution split whereby the distributor is expected to recoup their P&A spend directly from their share of the net rental. For instance, on a 70/30 split, 70% of the net rental would go to the distributor and they would have to recoup all their P&A costs from that sum, while 30% would be remitted to the producer or sales agent.

Gross receipts: also known distributors' net rental, i.e. the amount remaining from gross box office after the exhibitor's share has been deducted.

Hold-over: when an exhibitor decides to extend the run of a film beyond its original expected playdate as a result of the film performing relatively strongly against the competition.

Hollywood Majors: the American studios MGM, Paramount, Sony (Columbia Tri-Star), 20th Century Fox, Universal, Walt Disney and Warner Bros.

House nut: the weekly overhead costs of a cinema.

In competition/ out of competition: refers to official selections within certain festivals. In competition means films will compete for prizes and therefore may be more critically examined. Out of competition usually indicates that the film will be screened, but that it is not competing for a prize.

Independent distributor: a film distributor not affiliated with the US majors.

International distributor: a company buying pictures, which buys films from international sales agents, which it will subsequently distribute in a specific territory. However, on occasion, this term is loosely used to describe an international sales agent.

International sales agent: a person or company who sells or licenses international distribution rights to distributors. Also known as sellers.

Inter-negative: a negative duplicate of a film made to protect the original film negative and inter-positive. It is used for printing multiple copies of the release prints.

Key art: the main design used in posters and advertisements for a film.

Lead time: the period between the press deadline and the date of publication of the magazine or newspaper.

Letter of credit: banking and financing term whereby a producer secures a letter from a reputable distributor or sales agent guaranteeing payment of certain monies at a specified time. Certain banks and financial institutions will then lend money against this document.

Licences: the process by which a sales agent grants a distributor rights to handle a film for a specified period.

Mainstream: used to describe a film of broad commercial appeal. They are targeted to attract large audiences both at a domestic and international level.

Marketability: the testing of the effectiveness of the marketing tools for the film.

Merchandising: the manufacturing, distribution, licensing and sale of items such as T-shirts, CDs and toys which use the names or characters of a film

Minimum guarantee: the funds that a distributor commits to the producer or sales agent for specified distribution rights in advance of the film's release.

Move-over: refers to the cinema which will continue to play a certain film during its run when it switches from a larger seating capacity to a smaller one. This can be within a multiplex or from one single screen cinema to another.

Multiplex: a type of cinema that comprises two or more screens using the same lobby, ticket sales and concession stands. It is often located close to large shopping centres, providing easy access by road and allowing the consumer to combine cinema going with other activities.

Negative pick-up: when a distributor or international sales agent acquires specific rights to a film from an independent producer without having had a prior financial involvement in the development of the project.

Net rental: the percentage of the gross revenues of a film that the exhibitor pays to the distributor. Also known as gross receipts.

One-sheet: the size of international film posters, (685mm x 1016mm). It is the most common marketing tool in Europe, used outdoors or indoors (e.g. in theatre lobbies). It contains a graphic design such as a photograph or a drawing, the title of the film with a special artwork treatment, the credits with the name of the director, the producer and the principal cast and crew. It may also comprise a copyline or good quotes from critics.

Opinion formers: people who are influential in spreading word of mouth on a film. They may be those working within the industry (distributors, exhibitors, producers etc), the media or the general public.

Output deal: the agreement between a distribution company and a sales company or a producer that gives the distributor the rights to a number of films over a period of time.

Overages: additional revenues paid by the distributor to the sales agent and the producer (according to an agreed formula) once the distributor has recouped their distribution fee and the minimum guarantee.

Pay-TV: a form of television in which the consumer pays a monthly fee to a broadcaster in order to receive the transmission signal as opposed to free-TV which can be received without payment, (excluding state licence fees) or special equipment.

Percentage deal: the split of gross receipts between the distributor, the exhibitor and other parties.

Pitching: a presentation of a film project by the producer or sales agent, usually made during the development phase and designed to convince potential investors to commit to the project.

Platform release: when a film opens in a limited number of cinemas in order to build word of mouth. Once the film has established its core audience, the release is widened to other cinemas in one or several waves.

Playability:	the process of testing how well a film is expected to perform among its target audience.
Playdate:	the date of release of a film in a specific market.
PMT:	photo mechanical transfer, also known as a bromide. Usually used for converting line artwork (i.e. titles styles and text) into an element which when given to a printer can be duplicated or combined with poster artwork for printing.
Positioning:	the process by which a film is positioned in the marketplace so that it will appeal to its target audience (be they financiers, distributors, exhibitors or the general audience). This can be achieved by using specific marketing tools such as advertising, publicity or promotion.
Poster-ready artwork:	once a poster design has been completed it is broken down into two separate sections. The visual design is converted into a textless transparency, so that it does not have any of the credits or titles on the transparency. The text and credit block is made into a PMT. These elements combined would be given to a printer to print the required number of posters.
Pre-production:	the earliest stage of filming which includes the setting of the shooting locations, the preparation of the cast and crew, storyboards, finalising the budget, and the shooting script. It precedes the principal photography.
Pre-sales:	funds raised by a sales agent or a producer for the financing of a film before it is completed.
Press attaché:	the publicity person hired by the producer, distributor or sales agent to secure media coverage on a film. Provides similar role as a unit publicist when the film is being shot, but a press attaché is often hired throughout the post production period and at certain festivals.
Press kit:	basic publicity material given to the media which usually includes cast and crew list, production credits, production notes, stills, biographies and filmographies of the cast, director and producer.
Press tour:	the process of sending the director and the stars out on tours to the major cities of a specific territory to promote the film and meet with the local journalists.
Primary audience:	the core audience of a film.
Principal photography:	the actual shooting of the film.
Prints and Advertising (P&A) budget:	a budget that covers the cost of releasing a film. It comprises the cost of prints, advertising, media spend, publicity and promotion. In the US, it also includes the cost of market research.
Prints:	positive copies of a film given to cinemas for the theatrical release.
Release advertising:	the advertising spend committed from the inception of the ad campaign to the date of release. Any subsequent expenditure is referred to as the continuation spend.

Reporting: the process of giving a detailed report of the money earned by a film at individual cinemas. Each cinema chain or cinema operator has to submit such a report to the distributor of the film. It forms the basis of allocating revenues between the exhibitor, the distributor, the producer and any other parties involved in the financing of the film.

Rough cut: an early edited compilation of a film assembled in the editing stage. It usually has a temporary soundtrack, but no opticals, effects, or titles.

Royalty report: financial accounting report supplied by the sales agent to the producer detailing the monies received and commissions and expenses incurred. Usually supplied quarterly.

Sales: the licensing of rights by a sales agent (the seller) to a distributor (the buyer).

Sales house: a company responsible for the sale of cinema advertising, in cases where the cinema circuit does not handle this process itself.

Secondary audience: a segment of the potential cinema audience which may be interested in a particular film, but may only be persuaded to go to see it after it has received favourable, and widespread, word-of-mouth and has been the subject of a skilful marketing campaign.

Sell-through: the purchase of videotapes by the consumer.

Servicing: the on-going delivery of post production materials by the sales agent or producer to the distributor, including such items as prints, publicity materials and trailers.

Shelf life: the finite time in which a sales agent or producer has to sell their film before it starts to lose its market value.

Showreel: a précis of the film on video tape or 35mm film, which often offers a more comprehensive taste of the film than a trailer. It is put together by the sales agent or producer with the first footage of the film and is usually 5-15 minutes in length. A temporary music track will often be used to accompany the showreel.

Star junkets: a press trip where a group of selected journalists are invited by a production company or a sales or a distribution outfit to a location where a film is being shot, so that they can meet with the stars and director for photo sessions and interviews. Also known as press junkets.

Sub-distribution: the practice of a sales agent hiring a local company in a specific territory to handle certain ancillary sales such as video or television. It also refers to the hiring of a distributor by a primary distributor for the release of a film in a limited geographical territory. It can be detrimental to the producer as it will entail double distribution fees.

Synopsis: a written summary of a script or of a completed film.

Taglines: copylines on posters emphasising particular aspects of the story.

Talker screenings: preview screenings designed to create and spread word of mouth and awareness on a film. Particularly aimed at the primary audience target of the specific film.

Teaser trailers: short trailers of 30 seconds maximum which use a combination of footage from the film, still photography and graphics. Their aim is to give the audience a very brief glimpse of the film and to arouse their curiosity.

Theatrical: related to theatres or cinemas. A distributor who buys the theatrical rights of a film is entitled to exhibit it in cinemas.

Tie-ins: promotional campaigns arranged in conjunction with the media or retail outlets to support the release of a film. It can include competitions in newspapers or promotions on specified goods which are combined with images or merchandise from a film or characters within a film.

Tracking: for a distributor, tracking consists of seeking out at the earliest possible stage any title that could be a possible acquisition.

Trade listings: published in the bumper issues of trade publications in advance of each market, they comprise a comprehensive list of the sales agents attending the markets together with brief details of the films on sale.

Trade papers: industry magazines published on a daily, weekly or monthly basis which are devoted to business coverage of the film, TV and video sectors. Examples include Variety, Screen International, Le Film Français and Cinema d'Oggi.

Trailer: a specialised marketing tool that allows the consumer to sample the film and which creates awareness of the title. Using clips from the film, and/or graphic styles for the titles and credits, the running time of the full-length trailer can be between 90-180 seconds.

Unit photographer: supervised by the unit publicist, the unit photographer is responsible for delivering black-and-white stills and colour transparencies of the film during its shooting.

Unit publicist: an individual attached to the pre-production and production stages of a film to handle press and publicity.

Video on demand: service delivered to the consumer by fibre optic or telephone line which gives the public the possibility to choose from a vast array of programmes via switched services.

Volume discount: reduced prices which can be obtained by distributors from servicing companies in return for guaranteeing them a certain level of work.

Vox pops: in the context of film marketing, this refers to a technique used for radio advertising of films in which live interviews with enthusiastic cinema goers are mixed with voice-overs or music.

Want to see: this denotes the desire of the audience to pay to see a film, as opposed to them simply being aware of the existence of the picture.

Window: the specified amount of time between the exploitation of various media rights. For instance, if there is a holdback of 18 months between the first day of theatrical release and the first day of video release, the window is 18 months.

Word of mouth: a term used to describe the general perception of a film among the public and media. Strong word of mouth is a vital ingredient in helping a film achieve box office success, while poor word of mouth will seriously hamper the film's commercial prospects.

INDEX

THE AUTHORS

JOHN DURIE

John Durie was born in Canada, completed his Masters of Science degree in film studies in the United States, and has worked in the international film industry since 1980. He is based in the UK.

Prior to setting up his own company, Strategic Film Marketing, he held a number of senior industry positions including Managing Director (UK Theatrical) and Director of Marketing for Manifesto Film Sales, and Head of Sales and Marketing for The Sales Company. He has also co-ordinated selected publicity and marketing campaigns for distributors including Columbia Pictures and Warner Brothers.

He has been responsible for the creation and implementation of sales, marketing and/or distribution campaigns for over 50 feature films including Barton Fink, Bob Roberts, Farewell My Concubine, High Heels, Reservoir Dogs, and Wild at Heart.

ANNIKA PHAM

Annika Pham was educated at Nanterre University in Paris and started her journalistic career with the press agency AFP. In 1987 she moved to Rome where she became the Italian correspondent for the French trade publication, Le Film Français. She returned to Paris in 1989 to become the paper's international editor. In 1993, she moved to London where she works as a writer and researcher for various MEDIA Programme initiatives including the Media Business School and Espace Vidéo Européen. She also now serves as the UK correspondent for Le Film Français.

NEIL WATSON

Neil Watson is a freelance media researcher and writer. He has undertaken a wide range of research projects for the Media Business School, including the feasibility study for Ateliers du Cinéma Européen (ACE), as well as work for a wide variety of other clients. He has held senior editorial positions for publications including European Media Business & Finance, the Hollywood Reporter and Screen International.